CW01652124

Penguin Garden Centre Guides

Beat Garden Pests and Diseases

Stefan Buczacki

PENGUIN BOOKS

Penguin Books Ltd. Harmondsworth. Middlesex. England
Viking Penguin Inc.. 40 West 23rd Street. New York. New York 10010. U.S.A.
Penguin Books Australia Ltd. Ringwood. Victoria. Australia
Penguin Books Canada Ltd. 2801 John Street. Markham. Ontario. Canada L3R 1B4
Penguin Books (N.Z.) Ltd. 182–190 Wairau Road. Auckland 10. New Zealand

First published 1985

Edited and designed by Robert Ditchfield Ltd
Illustrated by Elaine Franks

Acknowledgements
The publishers would like to thank the following contributors and copyright owners of the colour photographs:
B & B Photographs (5. 13. 20 above and below. 21. 24. 25. 28. 32. 36. 37. 41 above and below. 44. 45. 49. 53. 57): Roger Cragg (29): Diana Saville (12. 16).

Printed and bound in Italy by New Interlitho, Milan

Typesetting by Keyspools Ltd
Colour separation by RCS Graphics Ltd

Contents

		Page
1.	The Causes of Garden Problems	4
2.	The Remedies – Cultural	6
3.	The Remedies – Chemical	8
4.	Trouble-shooting Charts – the Key	10
5.	House Plants	12
6.	Seed and Seedlings	14
7.	Bedding Plants. Nutritional Disorders	16
8.	Herbaceous Perennial Plants	18
9.	Trees and Shrubs	22
10.	Fruit Trees	26
11.	Soft Fruit	32
12.	Vegetable Fruit	36
13.	Leafy Vegetables	42
14.	Root Vegetables	46
15.	Problems in Greenhouses	50
16.	Storage Problems with Fruit and Vegetables	52
17.	First Aid	54
18.	Traditional Remedies	58
19.	Pest and Disease Spraying Calendar	60
	Index	62

1. The Causes of Garden Problems

Plants, like people and animals, are living organisms. The advice one gives to children with pets – 'take good care of them' – is worth remembering by gardeners therefore, for, like people and animals, plants will only remain and grow in a healthy manner if they are properly looked after. Neglect and unhygienic practices will lead to disease and pest infestation in the garden, just as they will in the home.

Before attempting to control or even prevent such problems, it is always sound to try and appreciate the nature of the cause, to endeavour to know the enemy. By understanding what the enemy is and how he sets about achieving his ends, we shall be in a much better position to choose remedial or avoiding action and, indeed, to appreciate why certain apparently sensible courses of action will not, in practice, have any effect.

Diseases

A disease, in the horticultural context, may be defined as a malfunction of a plant brought about by some organism that cannot be classed as a member of the animal kingdom. In practice, this means a fungus, bacterium, or virus (and I include among the latter those organisms once thought viruses but now known to be rather different, although comparably minute and referred to as mycoplasmas or other virus-like organisms). Neither fungi, bacteria nor viruses are now considered members of the plant kingdom, each having its own, unique grouping. None of them possesses the green colouring-matter, chlorophyll, that enables plants to manufacture their own food substances from the raw materials of carbon dioxide and water. Thus these organisms must obtain their nutrition in other ways and they do this by feeding on the organic materials contained in other living things, both plant and animal.

Those fungi and bacteria that feed solely on dead matter are known as saprobes and those that feed on still-living matter are called parasites. When the parasitic activity gives rise to the symptoms of disease, the organism is known as a pathogen. Whilst those fungi and bacteria that live parasitically are the main concern of this book, it should be remembered that the hundreds of saprobic species are of vital importance in the garden too, for they are the means by which compost and other organic remains are broken down and the chemicals contained in them returned to the soil as plant food. The heat that is generated in a well-built compost heap is the result of the chemical processes undergone during the decomposition. Nor should it be imagined that the division into saprobe and parasite is a water-tight categorisation, for many fungi and bacteria are capable of existing in either state. Indeed, it is the ability of a particular pathogen to live in innocuous fashion on dead organic matter and then turn its attention to living tissue that underlines the importance of garden hygiene, discussed on page 7. Nonetheless, some fungi and bacteria, generally considered to be more specialised and, perhaps, more advanced in an evolutionary sense, cannot survive in the absence of a living plant (termed the 'host' of the pathogen). Familiar examples of these specialised pathogens include rusts and mildews, whereas other equally familiar and troublesome problems like botrytis grey mould are much less specialised and are as at home on piles of dead vegetation as they are on living plants.

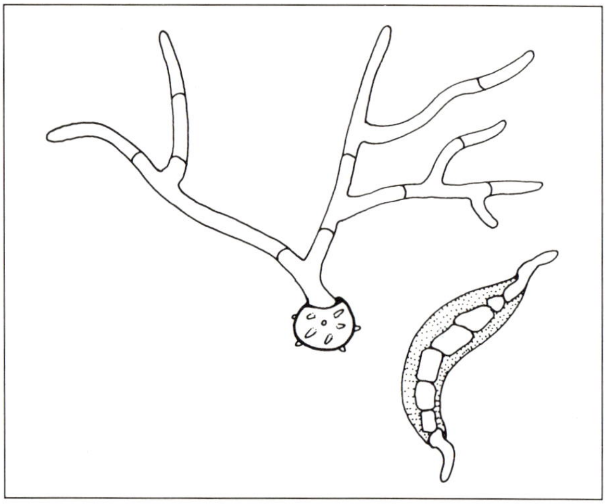

Germinating fungal spores magnified × 5000 approx.

Viruses are quite different biologically from either fungi or bacteria. They are all highly specialised and can exist only within the living cells of another organism with which they form an intimate parasitic relationship. Moreover, whereas the growth of fungi can be seen *en masse* (with the larger forms, such as toadstools, each individual organism can be seen distinctly, and even the single-celled bacteria are rendered apparent as coloured droplets, each containing millions of separate entities), viruses are quite invisible to the naked eye. Indeed, they are quite invisible with a conventional microscope; complex and powerful electron microscopes, capable of magnifying many thousands of times, are needed.

Most of the important diseases of man are caused by viruses, with bacteria a close second and fungi a fairly insignificant third. The reverse tends to be true of plants and most of the diseases described in this book are caused by fungi. To help understand some of the control measures outlined in the following pages, therefore, it is important to appreciate two features of the life history and biology of fungi. Firstly, they are very prone to damage by drying out and are, by and large, not able to grow and feed at low temperatures – a feature of our winters and a problem compounded for parasites by the fact that their host plant has very probably died down itself to some form of perennating body – a rootstock, corm or seed for instance. Thus, during the winter, fungi are in a vulnerable condition and are not in a position to spread and disperse rapidly. The second feature of fungi that should be realised is that implied by the last statement; they are, during their active growth in the summer, able to multiply and disperse very rapidly indeed. They do this by their method of reproduction which produces, not seeds, but spores; much smaller, relatively fragile bodies that are easily blown by the wind, germinate and grow into new organisms very quickly and whose formation should be prevented at all costs.

Pests

Pests, by definition, are members of the animal kingdom that bring about malfunctions of plants. They are an enormous and diverse group of creatures representative of most of the main subdivisions of the kingdom and ranging in size from microscopic eelworms to red deer! Unlike many of the organisms that cause diseases, pests at least have the inherent advantage that it is usually possible actually to see your enemy, if not always to look him in the eye.

With such a wide range of animal types, it is difficult to generalise over the way in which their biological features are of importance in bringing about the damage that they cause. Nonetheless, the broad division into sucking creatures and chewing creatures is one that holds reasonably true, the latter, including beetles, caterpillars and squirrels, contrasting with the former which include a more discrete assemblage of such pests as aphids, whiteflies and, appropriately enough, suckers. Whilst the chewing pests can quite quickly cause a considerable amount of damage, the size of the initial population is the governing factor. Thus whilst one rabbit can create havoc, one caterpillar, which will be unable itself to multiply while on the plant, is a much more tolerable proposition and even if it is allowed to continue unchecked, the ultimate amount of damage may be fairly small. Not so with many of the sucking pests, where the adult, rather than the immature or larval form, is often the active agent and thus will reproduce and multiply whilst on the plant. Miss the first few aphids of the season and there will very soon be hundreds, if not thousands of individuals to contend with.

Although I have said that pest species occur among many of the groups of the animal kingdom, there is no doubt that one group, the insects, outweighs all others in importance. More pests occur among the insects than among all other groups put together and they include aphids, beetles, butterfly and moth caterpillars, whiteflies, thrips and leafhoppers among many others. Most reproduce by laying eggs and passing through an immature or larval form which is very often the stage of the life history that damages our plants. In some instances both adults and larvae are troublesome; whereas the rapidly multiplying aphids referred to earlier achieve their population explosions by giving birth to living young. Among other invertebrate groups, pest species are found among woodlice, millepedes, slugs and snails (molluscs) and the microscopic eelworms. At the other end of the spectrum lie birds and, of course mammals, ranging in size from voles and mice, through moles and rabbits to deer.

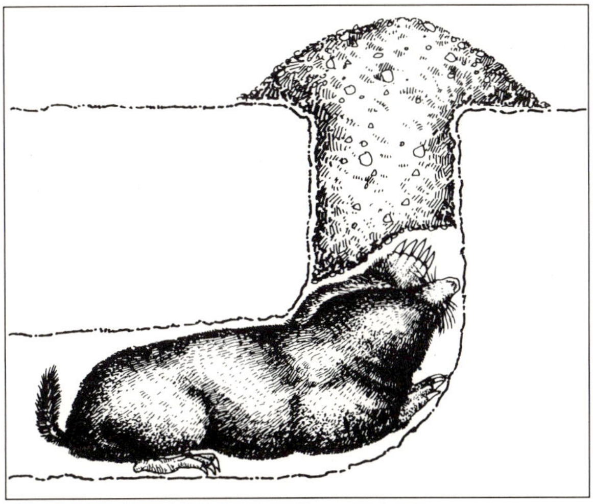

Moles are typical mammalian pests in their relatively large size and slow rate of reproduction. They are unusual however in causing damage indirectly and not by chewing or sucking plant tissues.

Aphids are, perhaps, the classically successful insect pests. They reproduce at a prodigious rate whilst on the affected plant and cause damage by their sap-sucking activities.

2. The Remedies – Cultural

Healthy gardens do not happen by accident. They are usually the result of a combination of sound and sensible horticultural practice, the way that the garden has been managed in the previous and earlier seasons, the soil and site conditions, the weather in any particular season, a fair measure of good luck and, possibly, a modern chemical control measure. It is not easy for a gardener to do much more than influence the first and last of these categories. The question of chemical control is discussed on pages 10–11, but whereas the existence of fungicides and insecticides is self-evident to anyone who strolls into any garden shop, the matter of what constitutes a sound horticultural practice and, more pertinently, how this influences pest and disease incidence, is a little more obscure.

Prevention is better than cure

Prevention is not only better, it is also cheaper than cure if the last resort has to be a chemical control measure. And pest and disease prevention can be effected in two ways; through the plant and through the garden environment in which they will be grown. It is essential therefore, when establishing a new planting, to obtain plants, seeds, bulbs or other planting material from a reputable supplier, for pests and diseases can be carried on any of these structures.

Plants in the form of transplant-sized individuals, crowns, rootstocks or young trees or shrubs should thus be inspected carefully and any obviously damaged or diseased parts cut away.

Seeds do not normally show visible signs of the diseases that they may be carrying, but a reputable supplier will always find it in his interest to ensure that his stock are derived from healthy individuals and have been prepared for packeting in as clean and careful a way as possible. It is highly improbable that, these days, in this country, you will find particles of soil or plant debris with the seed in a packet. It should be added, nonetheless, that the many gardeners who save their own seed would do well to try and emulate this standard of quality and, above all, only to save seed from individuals that are, themselves, vigorous and healthy.

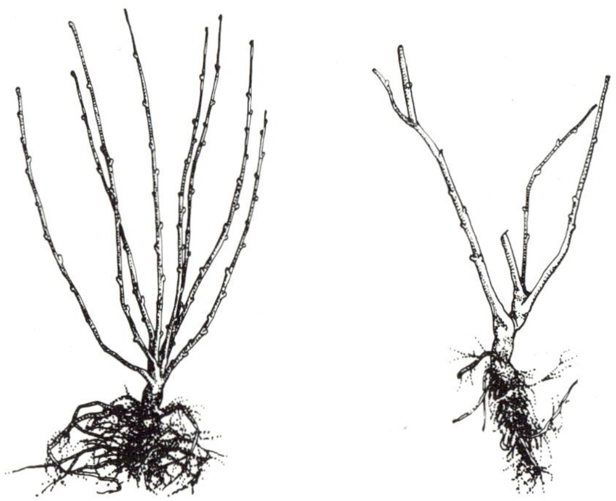

A strong plant purchase, and a weak one

Bulbs It is perhaps in the area of ornamental bulbs that most problems are encountered and the sale of 'job lots' of decidedly inferior quality daffodil and narcissus bulbs is something that regrettably still continues. Close examination of such bulbs will reveal not only that many are undersized compared with those from a well-known and reputable source, but many will have small surface lesions, indicative of a disease problem and may also have scarring or erosion of the surface as evidence of some form of pest attack. Once again, the gardener who lifts bulbs from his own garden is well-advised to sort out or 'rogue' his stock and throw away any showing signs of disease. The wrench may seem hard at the time but viewed against the likelihood of introducing contamination into an entire bed, the insurance policy is sound. And, with bulbs and corms, the insurance policy might well extend to the routine use of a fungicide dip.

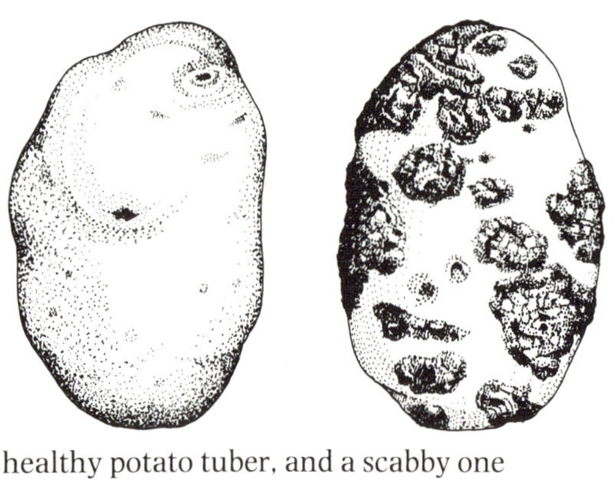

A healthy potato tuber, and a scabby one

Where seeds or bulbs, corms and tubers have been collected or lifted from the garden, there is a further factor to be considered, for whilst they may be perfectly healthy at the time of lifting, they can deteriorate whilst they are being stored. Cool, dry, well ventilated conditions are needed for bulbs and these are best supplemented by a dusting with one of the combined fungicide and insecticide dressings now available. Seeds are best stored in paper packets in a fridge.

Viruses and resistant plants

There is one group of diseases for which the purchase of healthy stock is of overwhelming importance. I refer to the diseases caused by viruses. The crops affected most seriously by viruses are those that are propagated vegetatively, that is by cuttings, bulbs, corms, tubers and the like, rather than seeds, for the virus contamination is likely to be present throughout the plants' tissues and thus to be passed on from parent to off-spring. The individual gardener can do nothing to rid any already contaminated stock of virus and this is one very sound reason why 'seed' tubers of potatoes are best not saved, but bought afresh each season and why such plants as dahlias, carnations and chrysanthemums should be examined most carefully before they are used for new plantings. With longer term crops such as fruit bushes and trees, the importance of ensuring that healthy stock is obtained is even more important. Always therefore, go to the most reputable supplier and buy only certified virus-free plants.

Mention must also be made of the phemomenon known as plant resistance to pests and diseases. Sometimes, plant breeders have been able to make use of the natural resistance that some varieties of some plants possess to certain problems. Where this is of use to the gardener, it iş mentioned in the text but it should be stressed that only rarely does it provide a complete solution.

A tidy garden is a healthy garden

Pests and diseases don't materialise from thin air, although they do seem to arrive in the garden as if by magic during the early part of the summer. Although some may have been brought in on the plants themselves, the garden itself and, most pertinently, the neighbouring gardens and surrounding area are likely to be the source of many more. Whilst relatively little can be done to influence events beyond your own boundary, a great deal can be achieved within your own garden.

First and foremost there is the simple matter of tidiness, for a neat and tidy garden is much more likely to be healthy than one that is cluttered with rubbish, debris and the remains of old plants. Those pathogens that can live saprobically or parasitically are one obvious reason, but it should also be appreciated that even those pathogens that can only exist on living plants are very rarely so specialised in their diet that they can survive only on one particular plant species. Usually, they can live equally well on a range of types, including many of those that will occur in gardens as weeds. Thus, a weedy garden is quite likely to be harbouring pathogens and, indeed, many pests too. What this does not mean, however, is that all natural vegetation must necessarily be cleared away. A natural balance is needed, for the quite simple reason that removal of all 'undesirable' vegetation will quite probably achieve the result that the widespread removal of hedgerows has had in the countryside at large. The natural habitats of the natural enemies of many of our pest and disease organisms have been removed with consequent freedom to multiply for the very ones that we seek to control.

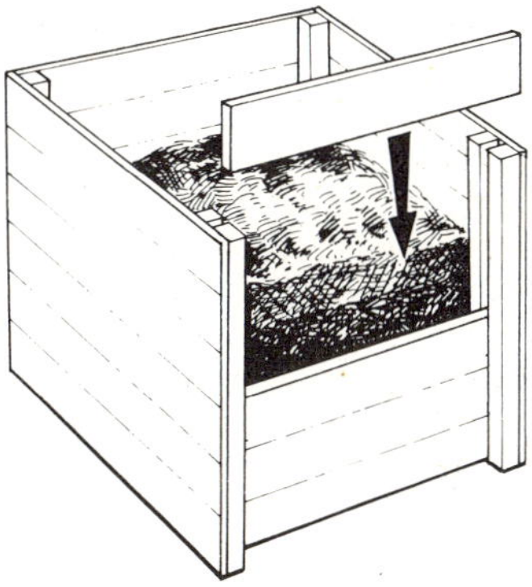

A bin for composting plant matter

An incinerator for burning waste and diseased plants

'Biological' control

In its best known examples, 'biological' control involves the use of small colonies of predatory species of insect or mite introduced into greenhouses where they will prey upon the pest species. Although this works fairly well in commercial practice, it is rarely as satisfactory on a small scale, largely because gardeners tend to grow a wide range of plants in greenhouses, and the use of a predator to control a pest of one means that no insecticides can be employed to control other pests of other crops.

3. The Remedies – Chemical

It is a sad commentary on the world in which we live that something from a bottle or a packet has become the first answer to a need or a problem. Modern medicine, with so many drugs and remedies so freely prescribed or on sale over the counter is but a part of this syndrome. As the majority of the population reach so readily for the chemical answer to their own ailments, small wonder that they apply the same principles to their gardens and drench the first sign of the smallest blemish with one of the dozens of sprays now available in every gardening shop. I do not believe this is the correct approach and yet I do not, by any means, subscribe to the so-called organic or no-chemical philosophy either. There is, as with most things in life, a median way. A thorough understanding of the principles behind natural control factors, behind sound husbandry and garden hygiene is a prerequisite for any gardener. Only when he has put all these into practice and still finds, as in many instances he will, that pest and disease problems strike, should he turn to 'the bottle' and let modern technology work for him. The British gardener is in many ways fortunate that the chemicals on sale to him through garden centres and shops, must, by law, have been cleared for use by the Ministry of Agriculture which will have been satisfied that thorough evidence has demonstrated the safety of a product, used as directed. The last phrase is the key one, however, for almost anything, including pepper and salt from your dining table, can cause harm if over-used or used in an unconventional way. Most of us know enough about pepper and salt to realise what is right and what is wrong. Very, very few of us however, know enough about garden chemicals to make such judgements and the guidance of the manufacturers must be adhered to strictly.

Nor should we seek guidance from the commercial plant-growing fraternity which uses far more of a far greater range of products than any gardener. Quite different criteria apply to commercial situations (whether or not they should is a quite different matter). The reasons for farmers and other commercial growers having available a different and larger range of chemicals may simply be due to marketing considerations (a particular chemical may not be worth selling in very small quantities) but it is frequently because its application needs techniques or precautions that are only accessible to the commercial operator; the product itself may not be intrinsically any more hazardous. The importance of this, nonetheless, is that gardeners must only use the products sold to them directly and should not seek products from friends or others among the farming fraternity who may offer other substances to them.

Insecticides and fungicides

Insecticides are chemicals intended to kill insects, whereas fungicides are those chemicals intended to kill fungi. Because the spectrum of pest and disease-causing species is larger than merely insects and fungi however, (see pages 4–5) the first and most obvious question is to ask about bacteria and viruses, about non-insect invertebrates and, indeed, birds and mammals. Most insecticides will have some effect on other living creatures – which is why we have to take precautions when handling them. Some insecticides will have some controlling effect on such pests as woodlice and millepedes but almost none will control mites or eelworms or slugs and snails. The latter are however effectively combatted with specific molluscicides, of which two are available to gardeners. Some fungicides will effect some control of bacteria but not very efficiently, whereas no chemical will affect viruses directly. Nonetheless, the impact of viruses can be lessened by chemical or other control of the aphids or other creatures which introduce them into plant tissue.

The gardener entering a garden centre or shop will see a very large display of both insecticides and fungicides on sale. How is he to make a choice from the up to 200 or so that are available? The first criterion is to appreciate that the actual number of chemical ingredients is only about a quarter of this total and the same substances are sold under several different brand names. Most advisory literature and radio and television guidance refers to the materials by their chemical, not their brand names. The same maxim is followed in this book and the chemical name should be sought on the product labels therefore; it will usually be in fairly small print.

It must also be understood that not all fungicides or insecticides will

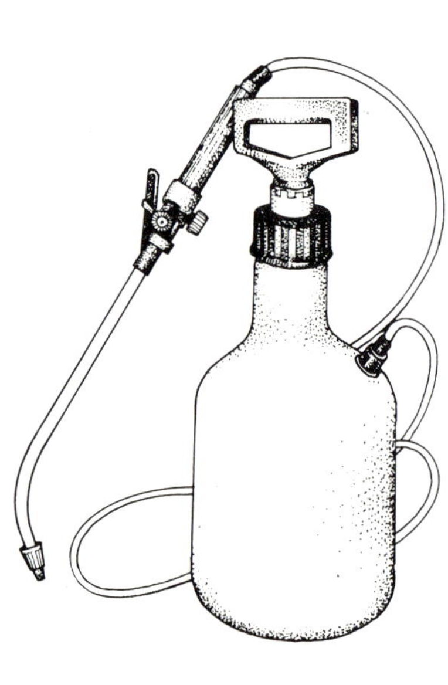

Pump sprayer

control all types of disease or pest with equal efficiency. Nonetheless, the average gardener will want to spend the minimum on garden chemicals and to make his life as simple as possible in not having to select from several dozen packets. Throughout the book, therefore, an attempt has been made not to list every possible chemical treatment, but to indicate where possible those products that will be active against the greatest number of problems. Although it is not suggested as a firm direction, therefore, most of the problems described in the book could be combated with at least reasonable effectiveness by a short list comprising products containing:

1. Either of the two fungicides benomyl and thiophanate-methyl.
2. A spray formulation of the insecticides permethrin, resmethrin or bioresmethrin; preferably in combination with dimethoate.
3. A dust formulation of the insecticide bromophos.
4. The molluscicide metaldehyde.

Hand sprayer

Systemic compounds

A word of explanation should be made also regarding the term systemic which will be found describing many modern garden chemicals. A systemic compound is one that is absorbed by the plant and moved in the sap from one part of the plant to another. By contrast, a non-systemic or contact product remains on the surface of the plant and kills pathogen or pest as the two come into direct contact there. There are advantages and disadvantages with both. The systemic product is required in smaller quantities, can be sprayed with much less accuracy (the plant itself ensures uniform distribution within), is not liable to be washed off by rain and have its effectiveness diminished, and is able to penetrate and eradicate pests or pathogens that are concealed and protected from more direct action. There are nonetheless certain disadvantages when edible produce is considered, for the very fact that systemic chemicals are taken up into the plant's tissues and have a long-lasting effect means also that the safe interval between time of application and the time that the produce may be eaten is correspondingly longer. In the vegetable garden therefore, a contact chemical is often the best choice.

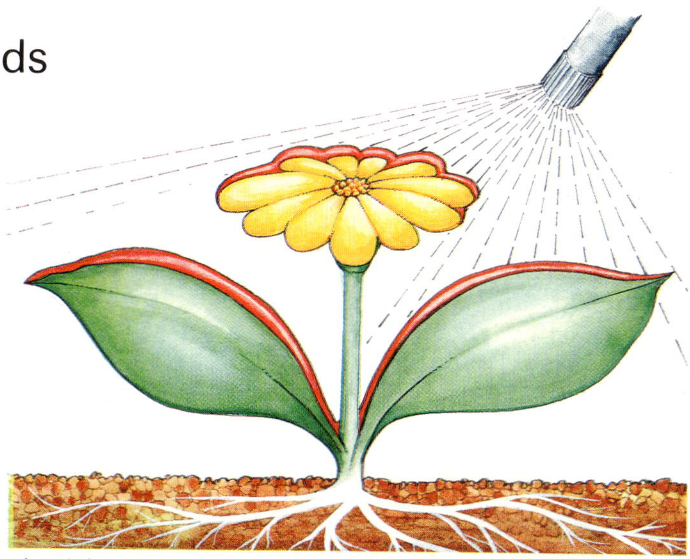

Applying a contact spray. Only the areas in contact with the spray are affected.

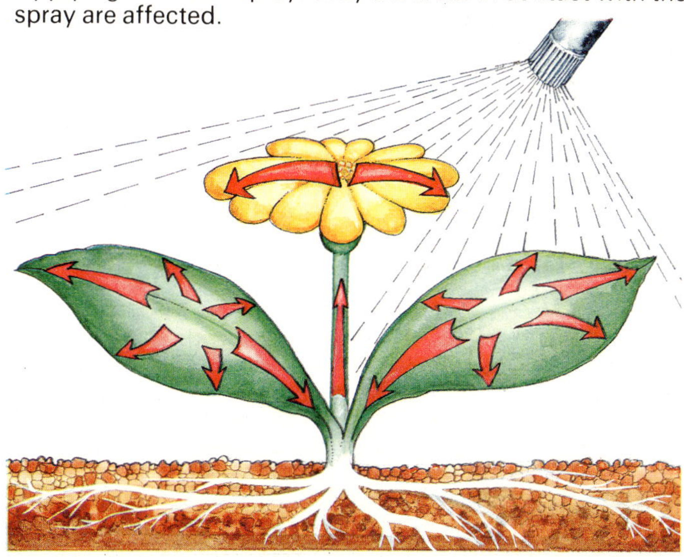

Applying a systemic spray. The plant absorbs the spray and carries it up its stem to other parts.

4. Trouble-shooting Charts – the Key

Identification is the key to successful treatment of any garden problem and there are several ways in which you can approach this. It should be borne in mind, nonetheless, that this book can only cover a selection of the many problems that can occur in gardens. Those selected are those most commonly met, but in some seasons, in some areas and especially on less common types of plant, others may be found.

One approach is to turn to the section of the book covering the group of plants with which you are concerned and read and check the illustrations to see if your problem matches any described.

A second way is to use the index where all the common plants are listed together with those of their problems that the book covers; if you are already familiar with the problem, this is an obvious shortcut. Even if you are not, the name will sometimes be sufficiently descriptive to give you a clue. Alternatively, you could check through all the problems relating to your particular plant.

The third, and most logical way is to use the Trouble-shooting Charts (not forgetting the First Aid section on page 54). The charts here will not, cannot, direct you to the specific problem for your specific plant; that would take many more pages. What they are intended for, however, is to guide you to the type of problem – mildew, aphids and so on, that your plant may have. Cross-reference to the index should then indicate whether that type of problem occurs commonly on your particular plant.

Problem	Detail	Probable cause
Symptoms on LEAVES		
1. Wilting	General	Short of water Root pest or disease Wilt disease
2. Holed	Generally ragged	Small pests (millepedes, flea beetles, woodlice) Capsid bugs
	Elongate holes; usually with slime present	Slugs or snails
	Fairly large holes over entire leaf or confined to edges	Caterpillars Beetles
	Semi-circular pieces taken from edges	Leaf cutter bees
3. Discoloured	Black	Sooty mould
	Predominantly red	Short of water
	More or less bleached	Nutrient deficiency Short of water Too much water
	Silvery (plums)	Silver leaf
	Irregular yellowish patterns	Virus
	Irregular tunnels	Leaf miner
	Surface flecking	Leafhopper
	Various (tomatoes)	See page 40
	Brown (scorched) in spring	Frost
4. Spotted	Brownish, angular, with mould beneath	Downy mildew
	Brownish, irregular or rounded; no mould	Leaf spot
	Dark brown or black; dusty	Scab
	Small, dusty, brown, black or brightly coloured	Rust
5. Mouldy	Black	Sooty mould
	Grey, fluffy	Grey mould
	White, velvety	Mildew
	Brown (tomatoes)	Leaf mould
	White, beneath leaves (potatoes)	Blight
6. Infested with insects	White, moth-like, tiny	Whiteflies
	Green, grey, black or other colour	Aphids
	White, woolly (indoors)	Mealy bug
	Flat, encrusted, like limpets	Scale insects
	Large, six legs, worm-like	Caterpillars
7. Curling	Insects present also	See 6
	Tightly rolled in spring (roses)	Sawfly
	Puckered, reddish (peaches & almonds)	Peach leaf curl
	Puckered, yellowish (pears)	Pear leaf blister mite
8. Cobwebs present	Plant wilting	Red spider mite

Symptoms on FRUIT

1. Pieces eaten away	Fruit close to ground	Slugs Mice
	Tree fruits	Birds Wasps
2. Distorted	With rounded bumps (apples) Black powder within (sweet corn) Ribbon-like scars (apples) Split (tomatoes)	Capsid bugs Smut Sawfly Short of water
3. Discoloured	Uneven ripening (tomato)	Virus Nutrient deficiency
4. Mouldy	While on plant (tomato)	Grey mould Blight
	While on plant (tree fruit) In store	Brown rot Fungal decay
5. Spotted	Tree fruit Tomato	Scab Ghost spot
6. Maggoty	Tree fruits Peas Raspberries	Caterpillars (Codling moth) Caterpillars (Pea moth) Beetle
7. Dropping prematurely	Pears Apples (in June)	Pear midge June drop (normal; not a pest or disease)

Symptoms on FLOWERS

1. Drooping	General	Short of water End of flowering period
2. Tattered	Masses of tiny holes Large pieces torn away	Caterpillars Birds
3. Removed entire	Usually discarded nearby	Birds
4. Distorted	Usually only a few plants affected in a bed	Virus
5. Discoloured	Powdery white covering	Powdery mildew
6. Mouldy	Fluffy, grey mould	Botrytis grey mould

Symptoms on STEMS

1. Eaten through	On young plants On older plants On young trees	Slugs or snails Mice or rabbits Rabbits or deer
2. Infested with insects	Green, grey, black or other colour White, woolly, on tree bark Flat, encrusted, like limpets Large, six legs, worm-like	Aphids Woolly aphid Scale insects Caterpillars
3. Rotten	At base; young plants On trees and shrubs	Stem and foot rot Decay fungus
4. Blister on bark of trees	More or less spherical Target-like	Gall Canker
5. Dying back	General	Short of water Canker or coral spot Root pest or disease
	Raspberries	See page 35
6. Abnormal growth	Like bird's nest Leafy plant Buds swollen (blackcurrants)	Witches' broom Mistletoe Big bud

Symptoms on ROOTS and BULBS

1. Decayed	General	Decay fungi
2. Parts eaten away	General	Small soil pests (millepedes, wireworms, leatherjackets)
	Corms and bulbs	Vine weevil
3. With irregular swellings	Brassicas and wallflowers Potatoes Peas and beans	Clubroot Eelworm Root nodules
4. Maggoty	General	Fly larvae
5. With warty spots	Root vegetables	Scab
6. Irregularly distorted	Root vegetables	See page 48

5. House Plants

In this section, ornamental plants commonly grown in houses are the subject matter. Ornamentals in greenhouses and all edible crops grown in greenhouses are considered on page 50, although there are a number of problems common to both types of protected environment. Almost certainly, the most frequent cause of house plants not growing satisfactorily is either too much or not enough watering. But as house plants are of so many different types, it is only possible to suggest reference to one of the excellent house plant manuals now available for guidance.

Diseases, with few exceptions, are not usually a problem on indoor plants; it is the pests that cause the anguish. The two diseases that occur at all commonly are the root and stem rotting that is a consequence of over-watering (which will clear up once the plant is allowed to dry out, unless the plant's demise is unavoidable), and botrytis grey mould. This ubiquitous problem can cause trouble in cool, damp conditions and is especially frequent on the crowns of Saintpaulias (African violets) when water has been allowed to splash onto them. Drying out followed by a drench with spray-strength benomyl or thiophanate-methyl is the remedy. It is worth mentioning too (especially as African violets are now so popular), that old leaves should be removed by pulling the stalks from the crown, not by snipping them off as this leaves short stubs through which rot will set in.

Any of the pests described below is likely to be found on almost any type of house plant.

House plants need care to keep them healthy and colourful.

Mealy bugs

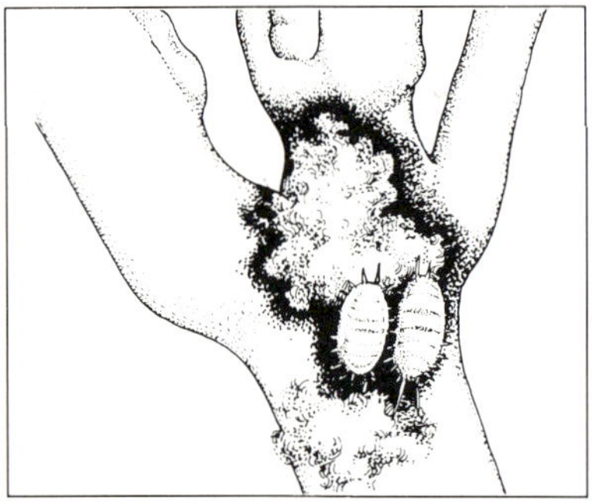

Recognition Small tufts of white 'wool' occur irregularly over the plants, although usually concentrated at leaf joints and in nooks and crannies. On cacti, they occur most frequently around the spines. On close examination, the white tufts will be seen to contain tiny pale-coloured insects that are superficially similar to woodlice.
Treatment Mealy bugs are notoriously difficult to eradicate. If a plant is severely infested, the worst affected parts should be cut away and destroyed. Exposed colonies can be treated by touching them with a small brush dipped in methylated spirits, but a systemic insecticide such as dimethoate should be used to spray plants with greater infestation. Several repeat treatments may be necessary.

Scale insects

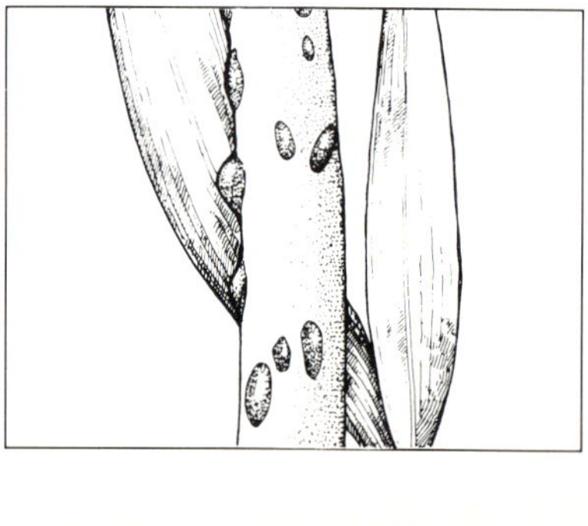

Recognition The problem with scale insects is not that they are likely to be mistaken for anything else, but that they may well be overlooked totally until the affected plant begins to decline as a result of their sap-sucking activities. They have been described as resembling brown fried eggs, mussels or terrapins although they are very much smaller than any of these! They occur most commonly on the stems and leaf stalks; less commonly on the leaves themselves.
Treatment Their hard protective 'shell' provides some resistance to most insecticides and, as with mealy bugs, a systemic chemical such as dimethoate is the most effective treatment.

Vine weevil

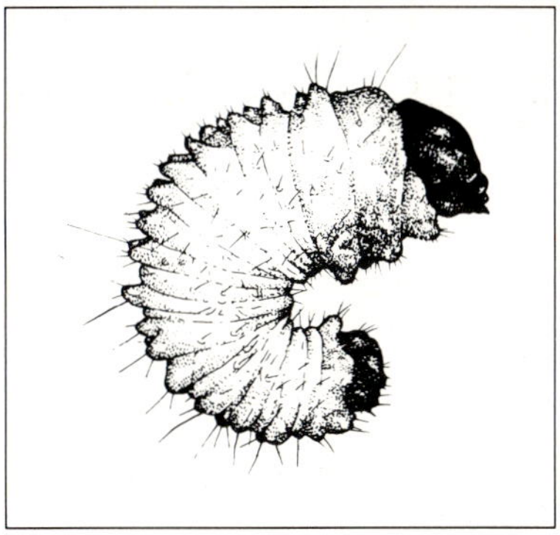

Recognition The immature vine weevil larva is the cause of trouble on house plants of all kinds, especially those such as begonias or cyclamen that produce large fleshy corms. It lives in the potting compost and eats its way into the soft fleshy tissues, sometimes causing the plant to die as a result. Although their holes are very evident, the insect itself is also frequently found. The larvae are white and legless and adopt a posture like that of the letter 'C'.
Treatment Any larvae found should be destroyed and affected corms dusted with HCH insecticide dust. The chemical should be used also when mixing fresh potting compost for begonias and cyclamen – dust a little into the medium before potting up.

Fungus gnats

Recognition Masses of tiny, dark brown flies will sometimes be seen on and above the potting compost of pot plants. Usually, there is no obvious damage to the plants themselves but the presence of the insects nonetheless causes concern.
Treatment Provided the plants are not obviously suffering, no direct action is really called for, but the presence of the flies should be taken as an indication that the potting compost has been allowed to become too wet and acid. Occasionally, the larvae of the flies which live in the compost, especially if it is a peat-based medium, may cause slight damage to the plants' roots, and in such cases they may be checked by watering the compost with a spray strength solution of the insecticide malathion.

Red spider mite

Recognition Red spider mite attacks are unmistakable, for affected plants become covered with a cobweb-like shroud within which masses of the minute mites may be seen crawling. Plants very rapidly wilt and shrivel.
Treatment Although on page 34 some suggestions are made for the possible control of red spider mite in certain situations where humidity can be increased, there is little merit in this for house plants. Control is very uncertain at the best of times, and it is far better to sacrifice the affected plant than run the considerable risk of mite colonies becoming well-entrenched in the house and infesting many other plants also.

Whiteflies

Recognition Small, white, moth-like insects fly up from plants when the foliage is disturbed; usually having been lying unseen on the undersides of the leaves. The plants become covered with the sticky honeydew that the insects excrete.
Treatment Although whitefly adults are susceptible to several of the modern insecticides that are available for house plants, the immature forms are not. Repeat treatments will be needed, therefore, to catch each fresh generation of adults as it matures. Take plants *outside* the house and spray them with either permethrin or dimethoate and repeat at ten day intervals.

Aphids

Unlike almost every other gardening situation, aphids are not the most common pests on house plants. They do occur, nonetheless, and should be treated by spraying promptly with any of the general house-plant insecticides now on sale. It is often convenient to use one with an aerosol formulation.

6. Seed and Seedlings

Whereas seeds are relatively robust structures, designed to survive adversity, (although, of course, quite likely to be eaten entire by the larger pests), as soon as they take in water prior to germination, they at once become more delicate and vulnerable to attack by pests and diseases of many kinds. The young seedling itself is even more vulnerable and must be protected in a variety of ways if it is to survive.

Damping off

Affects seedlings of all types, although certain forms of damping off are always more common on certain types of plant.

Recognition There are basically two types of damping off. In the first, the seed becomes infected and dies before it germinates, or, at least, before the seedling has emerged above the soil. The symptom here is simply a failure of the plant to appear. The second type of damping off is more apparent however, for the young seedlings, either in a seed box or a garden bed, die after they have begun to grow. Sometimes mould growth is present on them whereas in other instances the stem appears dry and pinched and the seedling merely shrivels away. Although damping off is, strictly, a seedling problem, the rotting of cuttings before they strike is brought about by similar causes.

Possible confusion with any pest, large or small, that removes and eats seeds after they have been sown. If the problem is extensive, it may be worth scraping away the soil to see if the dead seeds can be found. Whilst this is relatively easy however with peas, beans or cucurbits, it can be somewhat tedious with smaller seeds!

Cultural treatment In seed boxes, cleanliness is the key to the avoidance of damping off and can be summarised as follows: don't try to raise seedlings in boxes in garden soil, but, conversely, don't try to economise and re-use seedling compost; don't skimp on washing seed trays and pots before re-using them; don't allow seed boxes to become too damp (by leaving glass over them for too long for instance), and don't forget that young seedlings need light – it is most important not to leave them covered with paper for too long. If a patch of diseased seedlings occurs in a seed box, it is unwise to plant out any seedlings from that box, for they too are likely to be carrying fungal infection; it is much better to dispose of them and start again.

Much damage to cuttings can be avoided by ensuring that the medium used for striking them is well aerated; for this reason, it should contain a high proportion of sharp sand.

Chemical treatment Whilst the chemical sterilisation of seedling compost or soil is impracticable for gardeners (largely because none of the necessary, reliable chemicals are available to them), fungicides can be useful. The routine dusting of seed with a seed dressing containing captan and the insecticide HCH will give valuable protection at relatively little cost, both against damping off and certain insect pests. A garden disinfectant, such as Jeyes Fluid, should always be used to treat seed boxes and pots; but ensure that all old soil and roots are washed off first and that the containers are given a final rinse in clean water before use.

Cuttings may be protected by dipping them in a rooting powder containing fungicide.

Resistant varieties All types of seedlings are likely to damp off if conditions are favourable for the pathogenic organisms concerned, but annual bedding plants and some vegetables such as lettuces, brassicas and peas and beans are particularly prone. Soft fleshy cuttings, such as those of pelargoniums are most likely to suffer from 'damping off' rots.

Birds, mice and other rodents, cats

Affect seeds and seedlings of all kinds; they are liable to be damaged, uprooted and/or eaten.

Recognition The effects are usually self-evident and, in the case of seed-eating birds such as wood pigeons or sparrows, the culprits will often be seen in the act of theft. Mice and voles tend to prefer peas and beans and usually work unseen at night; as a result, their activities are often not suspected until the plants fail to emerge and inspection reveals that the seeds have vanished. Cats are more generally destructive, for their unearthing of seeds and seedlings is indiscriminate and incidental to their use of freshly disturbed earth for other purposes!

Possible confusion with some forms of damping off that bring about the death of seeds.

Cultural control Protection and prevention are the keys to control, for whilst small rodents can be trapped, this is to be discouraged in gardens because of the risk of injuring birds and domestic animals. Overall, the most effective method is to cover seed beds with wire netting; although a mesh as small as 1 cm will be needed to exclude mice. Cotton and similar materials may trap and injure birds and should not be used, although the various bird scaring devices are worth trying if they don't adversely affect the neighbours!

Chemical control The fungicide and insecticide seed dressing recommended against damping off will render seeds unattractive to rodents. Chemical bird and cat repellents are of very variable effectiveness and are really only worth trying if all else fails, for they are very prone to being washed away by rain.

Two points should be borne in mind; firstly, all birds are legally protected and, no matter how troublesome the problem, gardeners must not attempt to kill or harm them. Secondly, unlike birds and rodents, cats are domestic animals and one that is your pest will be someone else's pet. A tactful word to the owner may be much more beneficial than a campaign of vindictiveness against his animal.

Cutworms, leatherjackets, wireworms, millepedes and woodlice

Affect seedlings of all types. Wireworms and millepedes are also very troublesome in damaging potato tubers. Bulbs, corms and tubers may also be attacked by some of these pests.

Recognition Cutworms are caterpillars, leatherjackets are the larvae of crane flies (daddy-long-legs) and wireworms are the larvae of beetles, but the damage that they all cause is similar. Seedlings turn yellow and remain stunted or may wilt and keel over as the roots are damaged or the stem bases severed. Woodlice will also sever young stems but more commonly nibble away at roots, stems and leaves, causing a general weakening. Millepedes usually remain under the soil and damage roots or extend wounds caused by other pests.

Possible confusion with other forms of root damage such as that caused by slugs (below), and some fungal rotting diseases which also cause seedlings to wilt or keel over. Excavation of the soil around the roots usually reveals the organisms responsible; the dingy brown cutworm caterpillars and leatherjacket larvae or the rather horny, wriggling, yellowish wireworms. Many types of small creature will nibble seeds and seedlings, but millepedes and woodlice are the commonest and will usually be found associated with the symptoms of their activities.

Cultural treatment The general procedures that will help limit all of these pests are the regular and thorough cultivation of the soil to ensure that they are brought to the surface and so exposed to birds and other predators and, above all, the routine clearing away of garden debris of all kinds in which they can hide and breed. In no aspect of pest and disease control is it so true that a tidy garden is likely to be a healthy one.

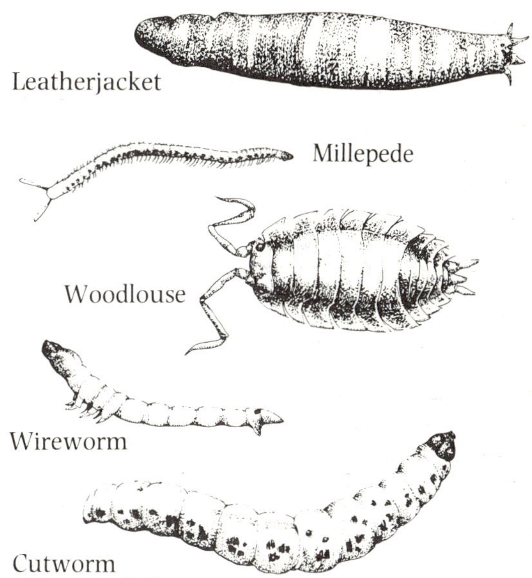

All magnified × 2.

Chemical treatment Although the routine dusting of seeds with a fungicidal and insecticidal dressing is a sound practice, its effects are likely to be confined to the seeds themselves and will not offer much protection to the emerging seedlings. Working HCH or bromophos containing insecticidal dusts or granules into the soil of seed beds should give longer lasting protection but this, too, must be combined with cultural measures.

Slugs and snails

The holes that slugs and snails eat into stems and leaves commonly occur in very large numbers, and result in an overall tattered appearance to the plants. The major clue to their activity, and the one that differentiates them from all other pests, is the presence of silvery slime trails. There are several products available for controlling them, but all contain either metaldehyde or methiocarb in pellet, liquid, powder or flake form. The major drawback is that they are all potentially harmful to domestic livestock, the pellets especially so. Vegetables and strawberries should not be eaten for at least two weeks after pellets have been used on them. Such substances as soot and ashes that are powdery and adhere to the slimy bodies of slugs and snails are fairly effective deterrents, and minutely spiny twigs such as gorse are claimed at act similarly.

7. Bedding Plants. Nutritional Disorders

The plants considered in this section are one step further on from seedlings, but they never build up the more or less permanent rootstock, bulb, corm or tuber of the herbaceous perennials. They include all the familiar, annual, summer bedding, the vigorously growing summer flowers such as sweet peas and the plants that, although strictly non-hardy perennials (such as pelargoniums), are more usually grown as annuals in this country.

A feature common to all these plants is the facility for rapid growth, but this is an attribute that can bring its own problems for the resulting tissues are intrinsically soft and prone to pest and disease attack. One most important way in which this can be minimised is by ensuring that the plants are well hardened off; accustom them gradually to outdoor temperatures before they are planted out.

Problems affecting plants in this group, that will be found described in detail elsewhere in the book, include soil pests such as cutworms, wireworms and leatherjackets (p. 15); slugs and snails (p. 15); mice, voles and birds (p. 14) – sparrows in particular are notorious at nipping off the flower buds; small, leaf-eating caterpillars (p. 42); aphids (p. 43); and powdery mildew (p. 44). The most important among biennial garden flowers are wallflowers, which can be affected by clubroot (p. 46) and by a problem known as winter killing – the death of plants during cold weather, generally thought to be caused by botrytis grey mould (p. 44). The major remaining problems of bedding plants can all be considered as establishment problems.

Root, stem and foot rots

Affect almost every type of bedding plant if the conditions are sufficiently moist but the most serious losses are probably with sweet peas.

Recognition The name is descriptive, for a rotting affects the roots, stems and/or the foot (the stem base) and may spread to cause the leaves and flowers to decay, the entire plant ultimately being lost as a consequence. Sometimes individual plants in a bed may be affected; on other occasions, an entire planting might fade away.

Treatment Because the causes of these problems are many and varied, there is no overall means either of avoidance or control. Nonetheless, certain general precautions may be taken. Even when plants have been carefully and correctly hardened off, as outlined above, they should not be given too great a transplanting shock; otherwise they are very much at the mercy of the soil fungi that are primarily responsible for the rotting, and of the pests whose initial activity may allow the fungi access to the inner tissues. Ways in which this transplanting shock can be minimised are by not planting into too cold or too wet a soil. Even at the end of May and the beginning of June, when many of the plants will be transplanted, cold spells of weather are not uncommon. It is much better to wait an extra week rather than suffer serious loss.

The plants should also not be under stress at the time of planting out. To minimise this, always ensure that they have been pricked on early into sufficiently larger trays or pots and that they are in an appropriate compost.

Pansy sickness

Pansy sickness is a very common but not fully understood problem affecting pansies and, sometimes, other forms of *Viola*, which quite simply fail to establish after being transplanted into a bed that has previously contained pansies. The problem is probably similar in origin to rose sickness and apple replant problems (see page 28). It can sometimes be circumvented by raising the plants in individual peat pots and planting them out in the entire block of compost which gives them a disease-free base from which to establish.

Nutritional disorders

All plants, of course, need feeding, and a fertiliser is essential to supplement the nutrients present in their growing medium, be it garden soil or compost. Nonetheless, of the plants described so far, house plants tend to be so cossetted and supplied with specially formulated liquid feeds that they never show signs of nutrient shortage, while seedlings and bedding plants grow so rapidly and are so short-lived that they do not have time to develop the more specific symptoms associated with the shortage of particular chemicals. This is not true of the remaining plants described in the book however, which are all either perennial or, in the case of vegetables, put on so much growth in such a short time that they can easily exhaust what is available. Although no attempt is made to give guidelines on general fertiliser usage, it is considered important that gardeners should be able to recognise the commoner signs of nutrient deficiency, if only to be able to distinguish these from genuine pest or disease problems. The following chart should help to identify the common symptoms:

What to look for – on leaves	**Plants commonly affected**	**Deficiency**	**Possible confusion with . . .**
—Pale coloured, often with tints of purple, red or yellow. The leaves are generally small and the whole plant may appear stunted. Effects appear first on the older leaves and spread upwards.	Brassicas and other leafy vegetables	Nitrogen	Root fly or club root – check that roots are not damaged
—Generally dull blue-green, sometimes with a hint of purple but not red or yellow. Older leaves are affected first and tend to be rather small; they may drop prematurely. Blackcurrant leaves become bronze.	Many different crops	Phosphorus	Root fly or club root – check that roots are not damaged
—Edges appear curled and brown or scorched, while brown spots may develop on the undersides. The older leaves are affected first.	Leafy vegetables, beans, tomatoes, potatoes and many fruits	Potassium	Cold or drying winds; salt spray at the seaside
—Tips of young leaves curled inwards and ragged or scorched. Central leaves of celery crowns are blackened.	Lettuces, celery, chicory	Calcium	Grey mould or boron deficiency
—Yellow between veins giving a marbled effect. Plants with red leaves may turn irregularly purple. Older leaves affected first.	Apples, tomatoes, brassicas, lettuce	Magnesium	Iron deficiency
—Bleached or yellow with veins remaining dark green. Youngest leaves affected first.	Rhododendrons, roses, camellias, hydrangeas, raspberries	Iron	Magnesium deficiency
—Yellow between veins of older leaves, often with dead patches too. Younger leaves more generally yellow and sometimes rolled upwards. Peas and beans have brown blotches on the seed leaves when seeds are pulled apart.	Beetroot, peas, beans, parsnips, brassicas, potatoes, spinach, fruit trees and bushes	Manganese	Several other problems, but manganese deficiency is most likely on wet, organic soils
—Leaves with imperfectly developed blade, giving a 'whip-tail' effect.	Cauliflowers	Molybdenum	None
— on fruit			
—Fruit small and highly coloured, combined with pale coloured leaves	Apples	Nitrogen	None
—Fruit ripen unevenly, some patches remaining green	Tomatoes	Potassium	Virus, but then patchy while still green
—Dark spots within flesh and on skin ('bitter pit')	Apples	Calcium	None
—Dark brown, tough patch at blossom end	Tomatoes, peppers	Calcium	None
— on vegetables			
—Masses of small tubers	Potatoes	Nitrogen	Calcium deficiency, but this also produces 'leggy' shoots
—Sprout buttons with dark internal patches	Brussels sprouts	Calcium	None
—Roots with black patches and rings in flesh	Swedes, beetroot and turnip	Boron	Similar effects on potato tubers are caused by cold or virus
—Curds with brownish patches	Cauliflower	Boron	None
—Leaf stalks cracked and pithy	Celery	Boron	Water shortage

How to correct deficiencies

NITROGEN	Apply nitrogen-containing fertilisers and manures regularly every season before planting. For very rapid response, use a liquid feed.
PHOSPHORUS	If balanced NPK fertilisers don't do the trick, apply superphosphate close to seeds or young plants.
POTASSIUM	If phosphorus and nitrogen levels are adequate, apply sulphate of potash before sowing. If not, then regular NPK application should correct the problem.
CALCIUM	Apply lime to bring pH up to 6.5. Cure apples or tomatoes by spraying fruit every two weeks with 0.2% solution of calcium nitrate.
MAGNESIUM	Scarcely worthwhile but if calcium is deficient too, apply magnesian limestone.
IRON	Do not use any lime. Apply sequestered iron as manufacturers direct.
MANGANESE	Cure affected plants by spraying with 0.15% solution of manganese sulphate.
BORON	Rake in borax (about 1 oz per 10 square yards – 34g per 10 square metres) at planting time.

8. Herbaceous Perennial Plants

Herbaceous perennials, for many gardening considerations, fall somewhere between the ephemeral annuals and biennials and the more or less permanent trees and shrubs. So it is with pests and diseases; the plants are there long enough for certain problems to build up over a period of time but not so long that they form permanent woody frameworks liable to be attacked by very slow-growing decay fungi. Despite these differences between annuals and biennials on the one hand, and woody perennials on the other, many of the problems to which herbaceous perennials are subject will be covered in detail elsewhere in the book and only notes are given on them here. This account concentrates therefore on three particular types of plant. Roses, although strictly speaking shrubs, are better treated as herbaceous perennials for much of their woody framework is removed deliberately each year. Bulbs and corms form a quite unique group with certain rather special problems, while lawn turf comprises probably the largest herbaceous perennial component of most gardens.

Slugs and snails

Although not usually serious on established plants, slugs and snails can be very damaging when the young shoots of dahlias, chrysanthemums and other herbaceous plants are just emerging.

Earwig on a chrysanthemum

Leaf spots

Spotting may occur occasionally on the leaves of most plants but it is only rose black spot that is likely to need treatment among herbaceous perennials. The very common spotting on the leaves of hollyhocks is a symptom of hollyhock rust (see below).

Earwigs

Although they are not serious garden pests, the shiny brown earwigs are very fond of making a home on and in dahlia and chrysanthemum flowers where they can cause alarm if flowers are brought into the house and may also nibble the petals. HCH dust will control them but should be used in moderation for it, too, can be disfiguring to the blooms.

Mildew

Powdery white mildew growth is very common on many herbaceous perennials in addition to roses, but the general advice in all cases is to spray with either benomyl or thiophanate-methyl as soon as the first symptoms are seen.

Aphids

Rose aphids will be familiar every summer but different species occur elsewhere in the herbaceous border too, most notably on dahlias and chrysanthemums. Spray with permethrin or resmethrin as soon as the first infestations are seen.

Hollyhock rust

Hollyhock rust

Although rose rust is the most important disease of this type affecting herbaceous perennials, the rust of hollyhocks and related plants can be devastating in some seasons. It causes small orange dimples on the leaves which soon wither and drop. It is most important to look out for the first signs of the disease and spray promptly with the only effective chemical, propiconazole.

Virus

Dahlias, chrysanthemums and carnations, like all vegetatively propagated plants, are subject to virus problems which give rise to distorted leaves and flowers and poor growth. They are only likely to be seen on old plants or if gardeners have inadvertently taken cuttings from diseased plants; most reputable suppliers will sell only healthy stock. Any plants suspected of having virus contamination should be destroyed before the disease is spread to healthy individuals.

Soil pests

Like slugs and snails, other soil-inhabiting pests such as wireworms, cutworms and leatherjackets can be troublesome to young plants. They can be kept within bounds by application of bromophos or HCH insecticide dust to the soil (see page 15).

Carnations distorted by virus

Problems on bulbs and corms

Bulbs and corms are specialised stem or bud structures for the perennial survival of plants such as narcissi and daffodils, crocuses, snowdrops, tulips and many others. Their soft, fleshy nature, which they share with tubers of such plants as dahlias and rhizomes of irises, tempts pests of many kinds and also renders them highly likely to be infected by decay-causing fungi and bacteria. They are vulnerable, moreover, at two stages of their existence – when planted in the garden and after lifting for over-winter storage. It is impossible to describe or discuss in detail the many different pests and diseases to which they are subject, but some generalisations can be made and the notes regarding the storage of fruit and vegetables on page 52 will be found useful too. One significant difference from fruit and vegetables, however, is that they may safely be treated with insecticides and fungicides. Whilst well-dried bulbs and corms stored in bags or on trays should be safe from all except rodents, therefore, those corms that are stored in peat or tubers stored in peat, ashes or other favoured material should be dusted both with flowers of sulphur as a fungicide and bromophos insecticide before being laid down for the winter.

Most of the problems that arise on bulbous plants in the garden are the result of fungi from the soil, or possibly on the bulb itself, infecting through some small wound. Care in handling is a prerequisite therefore and, as a routine, they should be soaked for about half an hour in benomyl or thiophanate-methyl (spray strength mixture) before being planted. The soil around the newly planted bulbs should be dusted with bromophos to deter pest attack. It is most important to try to improve the drainage of heavy soils before planting and, with some types of plant such as lilies, the laying of two or three inches of sand beneath the bulbs is virtually essential if rotting is to be avoided.

Once the plants emerge, it is vital that they are checked regularly for signs of poor or abnormal growth and any affected individuals removed, preferably with a trowelful of the surrounding soil.

Rose mildew, blackspot and rust

To many people, these three, quite different diseases, are inseparable, all of them affecting roses in most gardens, although rust is the least common of the three. None of them is likely to infect other types of plant although related forms of mildew, rust and leaf-spot can, of course, occur on other species.

Mildew

Recognition It is unlikely that any gardener needs to be told how to recognise this disease, probably the commonest of all garden problems. It is rarely seen before May in most parts of the country. Climbers or other roses grown in dry, sheltered spots, such as close to walls, are especially prone to attack; the powdery white mildew growth is most obvious on the leaves, which tend to curl and take on a purple tint, but the infection can also spread to the flowers.

Cultural treatment Try to avoid highly nitrogenous fertilisers such as dried blood; balanced rose fertilisers are much more reliable and don't encourage soft susceptible growth. On dry sites always endeavour to improve the soil moisture retentiveness with mulches.

Chemical treatment See over.

Resistant varieties There is wide variation amongst cultivars in their susceptibility to mildew, and members of the Royal National Rose Society may obtain the most up-to-date information on the results of trials. Because new strains of mildew may arise, resistant varieties do not always remain resistant; the best example of this being 'Super Star', once highly recommended but now attacked severely almost everywhere. The following list indicates a selection of hybrid tea and floribunda types of different colours that are fairly reliable:

Red – Hybrid Tea: 'Alec's Red'; 'Champs Elysées'
Floribunda: 'City of Belfast'
Pink – Hybrid Tea: 'Blessings'; 'Charlie's Aunt'
Floribunda: 'Escapade'; 'Michelle'
Yellow – Hybrid Tea: 'King's Ransom'
Floribunda: ''Allgold'; 'Arthur Bell'
Mixed colours – Hybrid Tea: 'Peace'
Floribunda: 'Golden Slippers'

None of the above is a very recent introduction for it is unwise to select varieties that have not had at least a few years to prove themselves.

Black spot

Recognition Black spots on rose leaves first appear towards the end of May in most parts of the country and if allowed to develop unchecked, gradually spread to affect a large part of the leaf which turns characteristically yellow and may eventually drop. The flowering and overall vigour of the plant soon begins to suffer as a result.

Cultural treatment Because the black spot fungus survives during the winter on the shoots rather than the leaves, hard pruning will help considerably in limiting its impact; collection and burning of fallen leaves will not, in itself, make much difference.

Chemical treatment See below.

Resistant varieties Resistance to black spot seems to vary regionally even more than resistance to mildew, but it is the yellow flowered roses that suffer consistently more severely and among them the following are probably the most reliable, although even they may well need the benefit of some chemical protection:

Hybrid Tea: 'King's Ransom'
Floribunda: 'Allgold'; 'Arthur Bell'

Rust

Recognition The first signs of rose rust in the spring are small, bright orange pustules on leaves and shoots but these are usually overlooked and most gardeners will be familiar only with the yellow and black, pinhead sized powdery pustules that develop beneath the leaves later. The leaves drop more rapidly as a result of rust infection than they seem to do with the other rose diseases.

Treatment Any diseased leaves should be collected up and burned. As with mildew, the over-application of nitrogen-rich fertilisers can predispose plants to rust infection.

Resistant varieties Although a few varieties such as 'Arthur Bell' and 'Queen Elizabeth' are notably resistant, most types of rose are liable to be attacked and some, such as 'Fashion', can be devastated if chemical control measures are not adopted.

Chemical treatment of rose diseases It is important to consider the three main rose diseases as a group for few gardeners will want to buy a chemical that is not effective against them all, or at least, against those two that occur most frequently, mildew and black spot. The best are probably benomyl, thiophanate-methyl and propiconazole, though the latter is the only one reliable against rust. Most gardeners will also need a treatment against aphids and there are now available products containing both fungicide and insecticide; nonetheless, the fungicides that they contain may not be the best choice for disease control.

Rose pests

Although aphids have been mentioned and are the commonest of the pests of roses, several others can cause concern in some seasons. The leaf-rolling sawfly lays its eggs on the leaves and causes them to roll tightly early in the summer. A spray with the systemic insecticide dimethoate should check the problem, although may need to be repeated after two weeks to catch all the larvae as they hatch. If not too severe, the affected leaves may simply be pulled off and burned.

The rose leaf-hopper causes a fine white mottling of the leaf surfaces but routine sprays for aphid control should give a satisfactory check.

The leaf-cutter bee takes small, semi-circular pieces from the edges of the leaves but, although disfiguring, little damage is caused and no treatment is necessary.

Many other insect pests may be seen occasionally on roses but rarely to the extent that treatment is needed.

Problems on lawns

Lawns are unique among garden plants. The grasses of which they are composed are closely related to cereals and many of the pest and disease problems to which they are subject are similar to those that affect cereal crops. Nonetheless, because, unlike cereals, the tops are continually being mown off, the various foliage problems rarely cause significant damage. It is impossible, moreover, to separate individual plants within a lawn and the pests and diseases are essentially those of the turf community. Lawn problems that are likely to be significant in gardens fall into well-defined groups:

Establishment problems These are the difficulties that arise when a new lawn is sown (newly laid turf is likely only to suffer from shortage of water, not pests and diseases) and they are considered on page 14 together with the general problems associated with seeds and seedlings.

Dead patches of turf One dead patch of turf looks pretty much like another, and a measure of common sense is needed to determine the cause. Yellow patches that arise during dry weather are probably the result of leatherjacket activity (see page 15) and excavating a small area should reveal the insects. The best treatment is to water the patch thoroughly, cover with plastic sheet in the evening and collect up the larvae which come to the surface during the night. If leatherjackets do not seem to be the cause, ensure that chemical has not been spilt on the area (see the comments on page 8) and if this is improbable too, a fungal disease may be the answer. There are several such diseases, some occurring during wet weather in the spring, others in dry weather during the summer and some accompanied by pink or grey fungal growth. Apply a spray strength mixture of thiophanate-methyl after mowing; as a routine preventative against fungal attack, do not apply nitrogenous fertilisers after September as this can encourage susceptible soft growth.

Fairy rings More or less circular rings of toadstools and darker grass can occur on any type of short, cropped or mown grass. Many people welcome them; many people don't mind, but others feel that the appearance is disfiguring and should be removed. However, the removal of fairy rings is very, very difficult. The procedure is long and laborious, involves fairly unpleasant chemicals and is only partly effective; it cannot be recommended.

Moles One of the most emotive of garden problems, moles occur most seriously in lawns although they can be troublesome almost anywhere in the garden – and have even been found under greenhouses. It cannot be pretended that there is a fully reliable answer and, indeed, moles figure prominently in the folk remedies described later in the book. Leaving aside but not dismissing such suggestions, the choice really is between driving them next door with smoke cartridges ignited in the tunnels or trapping and killing them with specially designed mole traps; the efficient use of these is, however, a matter for the expert.

Lichen and algae Although strictly neither pest nor disease, the growth of lichen or, less commonly, the green slime of algae is a cause of concern. Their control is most usually affected by one of the proprietary moss killers based on dichlorophen but the presence of the growths should be taken, as it should with moss, as an indication that the lawn is in need of feeding, draining, possibly less close mowing, less shade and/or aeration.

It is difficult and often impossible to rid a lawn of this type of fairy ring.

9. Trees and Shrubs

Ornamental trees and shrubs share some problems with fruit trees, but as the group includes conifers and other evergreen species, in addition to deciduous types, a further, quite distinct group of pests and diseases may arise also. As trees and shrubs are, by their nature, 'long-term' garden plants, many of the problems that affect them are long-term also in that they attack and decay the woody fabric. This has the incidental advantage that damage from them does not occur very rapidly, and if detected sufficiently early extensive harm may be arrested. Nonetheless, three of the most devastating of all tree and shrub problems, honey fungus, phytophthora root death and fireblight are exceedingly difficult to control at any time.

Leaf spots

Almost every type of deciduous tree and shrub is likely to develop spotting on the leaves from one cause or another. The difficulty is to know which are serious and which not, but it is probably simplest to err on the side of 'leave well alone'. Relatively few leaf spotting diseases are likely to cause significant damage to well established plants: even those most dramatic in appearance, such as tar spot on maples, seem to have little effect. Only where an ornamental tree or shrub is really conspicuously disfigured should any chemical treatment be called for. Even here, recommendations are difficult to make because of the wide variety of causal agents likely to be involved, but two sprays with benomyl or thiophanate-methyl at three week intervals, should be at least moderately effective, if tricky to apply to large trees. Probably the only significant exception to this is the anthracnose disease of weeping willows, where tiny reddish leaf spots accompany the development of grey twig lesions and dying back of the shoots; overall, an excellent set of reasons for not planting weeping willows in gardens! The only chemical spray likely to have any impact on this problem is Bordeaux Mixture.

If the damage on the leaves can more accurately be described as holes, rather than spots, then the cause is likely to be insect, not fungus; see 'Caterpillars' on page 25.

Fireblight

Affects many trees of the rose family; especially pears, hawthorns, pyracantha, cotoneaster, amelanchier, apples and chaenomeles. This disease has been the biggest problem to strike the British fruit crop in recent years, first reaching this country in 1957 after being long excluded by strict import regulations. It is also a very serious problem on many ornamental plantings.

Recognition The effects arise dramatically and suddenly and give the appearance of the tree or bush having been scorched by a flame – hence the name. Dead blossoms hang from the branches and, when conditions are sufficiently warm and moist, drops of glistening slime cover the shrivelled flowers and leaves. Twigs, then branches and, finally, entire trees may die within a very short time.

Possible confusion with real fire damage! Fairly commonly, especially on hawthorn, reports of fireblight subsequently prove to be the result of someone inadvertently setting fire to a hedge with a wayward bonfire. On fruit trees, the effects of bacterial blossom wilt are discussed on page 26, but in recent seasons, mysterious death of ornamental cherries, especially of the variety 'Kanzan' has been reported from many parts of the country. The symptoms are superficially very like those of fireblight but this disease does not, in fact, affect cherries and the true cause is unknown.

Treatment Treatment of fireblight is by means of the telephone, for it is classed legally as a 'Notifiable Disease' and must, therefore, be reported to the local office of the Ministry of Agriculture. Ministry officials will then inspect the suspected outbreak and advise on the appropriate course of action – which will be either to fell or not to fell, for no chemical remedy is available.

Mistletoes and unusual growths

Sometimes, trees will be seen bearing large twiggy or leafy growths that appear 'out of keeping' with the remainder of the plant. They are most likely to be noticed in winter when deciduous trees are leafless, and take two main forms. Mistletoe is a familiar, evergreen, semi-parasitic flowering plant that buries a root-like, feeding organ into the trees. Many people welcome mistletoe on an old apple tree, and its impact on the overall vigour of the plant is likely to be slight. Even when the growth of the parasite virtually supplants the crown of the tree, such as occurs rarely in this country but which is common on old apples, poplars and other trees in France, my view is that the whole is an adornment rather than a disfigurement of the garden.

Growths will also be seen, especially on silver birch trees, that appear rather like leafless mistletoes or, possibly, large birds' nests. These are known as witches' brooms and result from some poorly understood malfunction of the tree's growth-regulatory processes. Like mistletoe, they too can be tolerated on garden trees and, from shoots of some types of broom (especially on conifers), dwarf varieties have been propagated.

Rots, decay, and wound treatment

Apart from the special case of honey fungus, many other wood-rotting fungi can cause damage to garden trees; but on the trunk and branches rather than the roots and thus, in many cases, restorative treatment may be undertaken. Any branch bearing fungal growths is likely to be extensively decayed and should be removed. If the decay is seen to extend into the trunk, it may be possible to gouge out the affected tissue but if it is clearly well-seated, the tree is better felled for it will be inherently unstable and likely to be blown down. In the cases of very large or valuable trees, professional advice and assistance should be called upon; partly because an experienced tree surgeon may be able to save them, but also because the felling of large trees is an extremely tricky operation.

When branches are removed, they should not be sawn flush with the trunk, as is often recommended, for this removes the natural wound-healing tissues. The branch should be removed as close as possible to the collar, the small raised swelling at the branch base. Doubts have been cast in recent years on the advisability of sealing cut surfaces with a wound sealant. It seems that the traditional, bitumen-like materials may cause more harm than good in preventing natural healing activity and possibly sealing harmful organisms into the tree. The debate continues but it does appear that the more modern substances containing the fungicide thiophanate-methyl are beneficial.

Root death (Phytophthora)

Affects almost all species of woody plant. This disease has supplanted honey fungus as their most serious killer in many parts of the country.

Recognition As with honey fungus, identification is not easy, but if all alternative, non-pathological causes can be eliminated, one form or another of Phytophthora root death is the most likely explanation of the yellowing and dying back of the foliage of ornamental trees and shrubs, especially of conifers, rhododendrons and ornamental cherries. If the roots close to the stem base are exposed, the older portions will be blackened while some of the young, fibrous rootlets are still white and living. The disease is most likely to be troublesome on wet, poorly drained soils although it does not occur exclusively on such sites.

Treatment The best answer to root death is its avoidance, which is best achieved by buying plants only from the most reputable nurseries or, if in any doubt, of buying only container-raised plants, which are much less likely to be infected. Thereafter, careful husbandry is essential as, once established in garden soil, little can be done, for none of the effective chemical treatments are available for garden use. Always slope the soil away from newly planted trees and shrubs, for any hollow that forms at the stem base will become waterlogged and create the conditions that the fungus requires. In heavy soils, do not excavate a discrete hole and fill this with peat, as this also is likely to become too wet. Always take care not to water, manure or mulch excessively.

Resistant varieties Whilst no woody plants can be said to be truly resistant to root death, it is among cypresses that most damage probably occurs; affected varieties can be replaced with Leyland cypress which, although less attractive than many, is relatively little affected by the problem.

Honey fungus

The black "bootlaces" of honey fungus under the bark of an affected tree.

Affects almost every species of woody plant, and damage can also occur occasionally on herbaceous perennials. Honey fungus ranks among the top three garden diseases in seriousness.
Recognition Most commonly, the first indication of the presence of honey fungus in a garden is the finding of a dead or nearly dead tree or shrub. Then comes the puzzling matter of whether or not honey fungus was truly responsible. If the tell-tale toadstools are present at or close to the base of the plant, the matter is relatively straightforward – provided the toadstools can be identified accurately! They are usually up to 6 in (15 cm) high with a cap up to 6 in (15 cm) in diameter; tawny or yellowish in colour with darker scales or specks towards the centre of the cap. Beneath the cap, the gills are white or yellowish and the stem usually bears a large, whitish, yellow-bordered ring. If the bark is peeled away at the base of the affected plant, whitish fungal growth or, more characteristically, flat, narrow, ribbon-like structures may be seen, whilst in the surrounding soil, objects similar to black bootlaces may occur. The fungus is less likely to attack old trees than young ones and is most unlikely to attack any trees or shrubs planted less than a year previously.
Possible confusion with a great many things! All manner of toadstools commonly grow at the bases of both live and dead trees. Most are quite harmless; some are positively beneficial to the plants. A good guide book to mushrooms and toadstools will help here. Decay in the trunks of trees more than about 2 ft (60 cm) above ground level is unlikely to be caused by honey fungus and the total absence of toadstools, boot-lace strands and fungal growth suggests strongly some other cause (see Phytophthora root death as a likely alternative).
Chemical treatment No 'conventional' fungicides have any effect on honey fungus and opinions vary over the effectiveness of proprietary phenolic emulsions. They are certainly worth trying as soil drenches to limit disease spread to other plants, but do not expect such treatments to cure plants that are already diseased.
Cultural treatment Sanitation is the more appropriate term here, for prevention of honey fungus spread rather than cure is the aim. Because the disease requires old stumps of broadleafed trees for its initial establishment, every effort should be made to remove the stump when a tree is felled. This removal should, however, be by physical means, as chemical stump treatments are most unreliable. Once a diseased plant is found, moreover, complete removal of it and its root system must be effected. Sometimes, further spread of the problem has been prevented by burying thick plastic sheeting vertically in the soil to a depth of at least 2 ft (60 cm) around the site of an affected tree or shrub; the same procedure may be useful if the source of the problem is in a neighbouring garden. New plants should not be planted on the affected area for at least one, and preferably two or three seasons, to allow the fungus to die away.
Resistant varieties Some trees and shrubs are fairly resistant. These include beech, box, many types of clematis, elaeagnus, hawthorn, holly, ivy, larch, laurel, mahonia, sumac and yew.

Mammals

Pests that can actually be seen in the act of causing damage are frustrating enough to the gardener. When damage arises mysteriously during the night, however, the anguish is compounded. This happens most frequently with trees and shrubs, especially in gardens close to fields or natural woodland. The shoot tips may be browsed or the bark stripped from stems and branches. Such damage may be caused by rabbits, grey squirrels or deer, and the only certain means of protection is by their total exclusion. To exclude deer, fences need to be at least 6 ft (1.8 m) high, whereas rabbit netting should be of small mesh and be buried to a depth of about 1 ft (30 cm). Squirrels are not excluded by such barriers and netting must be draped over plants. Trees or shrubs with an appreciable length of straight stem may be protected from bark stripping with spiral tree protectors.

Mildew

Although mildew is seen on trees and shrubs much less frequently than it is on herbaceous plants, it can be serious on a few species. Young oaks, sycamores, lilacs, laburnums and Japanese spindle are among those on which it is seen most frequently. As with all tree problems, spraying is impracticable if the plant is very large, but small specimens can be treated with benomyl or thiophanate-methyl.

Mysterious swellings

Trees and shrubs sometimes become infected with organisms that bring about the development of symptoms slowly and imperceptibly over a considerable period of time. Cankers fall into this category and can be extremely damaging if allowed to develop unchecked; they are described and discussed in the section on tree fruit problems. Quite commonly however, more or less rounded, woody swellings cause concern when first seen but rarely bring about any actual damage. They are believed to be caused by a type of bacterium and are sometimes referred to as 'Crown Gall'. Attempts to cut them out usually cause more disfigurement than they cure and they are best left alone.

Caterpillars

Some trees are much more prone than others to the attentions of leaf-eating caterpillars. Not surprisingly, those with large, soft leaves seem most likely to be devoured. It is never worthwhile undertaking routine protective spraying against caterpillars on garden trees or shrubs, but vigilance is needed to detect the first tell-tale signs of holing or chewing of the leaf edges. As with virtually all problems on large trees, it is impracticable to attempt to treat the whole plant, but with smaller trees and shrubs, one or two sprays with permethrin should take care of the caterpillars.

Coral spot

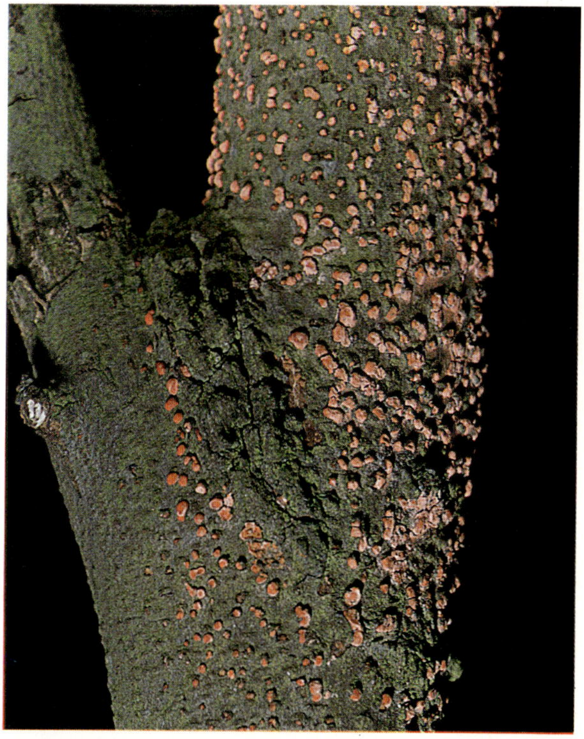

Affects most woody plants, although relatively uncommon on conifers. Coral spot is one of the most underestimated of garden diseases, although it is one that can be a killer.

Recognition Distinctive, pin-head sized pink pimples cover the bark of affected twigs and branches, which die back as a result. The same symptoms will commonly be seen in gardens on dead twigs and branches of all kinds and are traditionally to be expected on old pea sticks.

Possible confusion with small, coloured pustules on old, rotten wood in gardens (fence post and stakes for example); usually yellow but occasionally white or pink. These are, however, caused by a harmless organism, quite unrelated to coral spot which does not affect sawn timber.

Cultural treatment Whilst it is always true that a neat and tidy garden is more likely to be a healthy one, this is never more valid than with coral spot disease. Any piles of prunings or other branches and twigs must be cleared away promptly. As the coral spot fungus must first establish itself on dead twigs and branches before spreading down from them into living tissues of a tree or shrub, careful attention to routine pruning, paying especial attention to the removal of frost damaged shoots and to cutting away old branch stubs, will go far towards preventing the problem. Once the symptoms are seen on a growing plant, however, the affected parts must be removed promptly and burned.

Chemical treatment Although a preventive treatment for coral spot is neither feasible nor desirable, an affected plant should be sprayed thoroughly with benomyl or thiophanate-methyl once the damaged tissues have been removed, and the spray repeated once more in two or three weeks time.

10. Fruit Trees

All fruit trees grown in British gardens belong to the same family of plants, the rose family, and as may be expected therefore, they share some common problems. Apples, close relatives of pears, have more problems in common with them moreover, than they do with plums, cherries, damsons, and the other stone fruits which all belong to a different genus. None of the tree fruits is closely related to soft fruits which tend to suffer from a different range of problems although orchard trees are subject to such conditions as cankers which, in one form or another, are common to ornamental and forest trees also. Most of the common problems that arise when fruit is stored (see page 52) have their origins whilst it is still growing on the tree. Thus, care and attention at this stage will reap benefits later.

Winter moths

Affect all types of fruit tree and many ornamental trees and shrubs also.
Recognition Leaves take on the holed, tattered and generally ragged appearance that is typical of caterpillar damage. The buds, shoots and blossoms are also attacked and, on close inspection, the green or brown caterpillars will be seen, characteristically adopting the 'arched back' stance known as looping. The fruits are not attacked directly but the trees suffer after repeated attacks through the indirect effects of loss of blossom and leaves.
Possible confusion with other types of caterpillar which may occur on fruit trees from time to time. These are rarely of the looper type and rarely in the numbers of winter moths.
Cultural treatment The best basic treatment for fruit trees is the grease band; a specially prepared type of grease which is painted on the bark of the trunk in a complete band around the trunk about 4–5 ins (10–12 cm) wide and 3–5 ft (1–1.5 m) above ground level. It is important to use grease specially manufactured for this purpose or to use the greased paper strips now readily available; although the paper is difficult to apply to rough bark in such a way as to prevent the moths from crawling underneath it. Nonetheless, lubricating grease is quite definitely not suitable. The purpose of the banding is to trap the female moths; they are unable to fly and have to crawl up the trunks to lay their eggs. The banding should be applied in October.
Chemical treatment A contact insecticide such as permethrin or derris can be sprayed onto the trees immediately after the buds have opened in spring. Nonetheless, this should not be necessary if the grease band has been carefully applied.

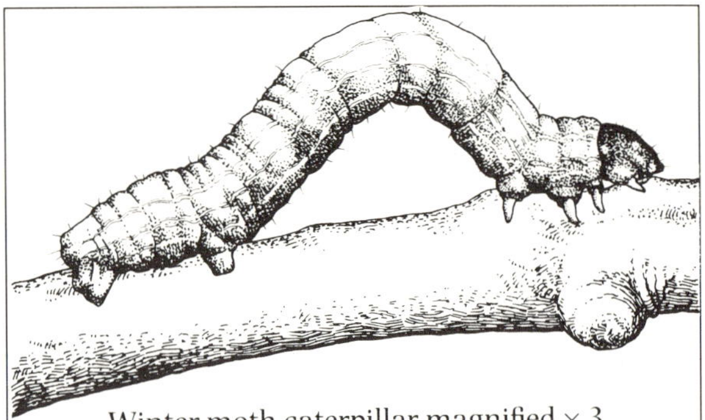
Winter moth caterpillar magnified × 3

Blossom problems

The splendid sight of a fruit tree in full blossom in spring should presage a bumper crop. Quite frequently, it doesn't. The reasons are sometimes readily apparent, especially when the fruit are seen to be attacked by some pest or disease. When the failure arises even before the fruit has set however, the matter is usually more puzzling.

Late frost is the bane of every fruit grower and is probably the commonest reason for a blossom failure. Nonetheless, frost damage is usually sudden and self-evident. The various blossom diseases need a little more detective work before they can be identified. One form of blossom wilt arises from the same cause as brown rot of fruit, the disease organism, in this instance, attacking the young flowers. The removal of any diseased fruit from the tree is doubly important, therefore; certainly none should be left hanging overwinter. On pears, death of the blossoms is more likely to arise as a result of bacterial attack; in its least severe form, the damage can be limited by cutting out and burning the affected shoots. Much more serious however, is the bacterial disease, fireblight, which affects many tree and shrub members of the rose family but which is consistently most damaging on pears (see page 22).

A small group of descriptively named insects called suckers live in, and feed on, the opening buds and blossoms (and also, to some extent, the leaves) of both apple and pear trees, resulting in distortion of the blossom trusses and consequent loss of the crop. Unlike the other causes of blossom failure, sucker infestations are almost always accompanied by sticky black masses of honeydew and sooty mould growth. Unlike the bacterial problems moreover, suckers can be controlled by chemical treatment: a tar oil winter wash will help to eradicate eggs overwintering on the bark, while a spray with dimethoate (three weeks after the petals drop on pear trees or at the 'green cluster' bud stage on apples) should kill the immature insects.

Viruses and certified planting stock

For many years, gardeners were puzzled when fruit trees began to decline in vigour and fruiting as they aged, for reasons that could not be corrected by normal pest or disease control or fertiliser treatments. Only relatively recently has it been appreciated that the cause is a build-up in the plants of invisible viruses, and only more recently still has it been possible artificially to free plants (or, at least, the 'parent' stock from which they are derived) from this viral contamination. Any reputable modern supplier of fruit trees will sell only virus-free stock and will be at pains to point this out in his catalogues. Thus, such stock must be the invariable choice when establishing a new planting.

You can know that a tree is declining through virus contamination by eliminating all the other possibilities, but sometimes there are also tell-tale clues. Although an expert eye is needed to identify many of these, the irregular, pale-coloured leaf patterns that virus infection often induces are quite distinct and unique.

Pear midge

Usually, the first sign of attack by pear midge is the dropping of the young fruits in early summer. If these are examined, they will be seen to be dark-coloured and distorted and to contain tiny, yellowish grubs. Pear midge can be a very annoying pest as certain trees seem to be attacked year after year (whilst those in neighbours' gardens seem to escape) and chemical treatment of the trees is difficult and unreliable. The most satisfactory procedure is to clear up and burn all the fallen fruitlets, and to rake HCH insecticide dust into the soil under the trees to kill the insects.

Brown rot

Affects all tree fruits, but is generally most conspicuous and severe on apples and plums.

Recognition In most seasons, almost every tree will have at least a few fruit affected and displaying the characteristic brown decay, usually with more or less concentrically arranged whitish pustules of mould growth. The disease spreads very rapidly by contact between diseased and healthy fruit.

Possible confusion with several other rotting diseases, such as botrytis grey mould which can affect fruit while they are still on the tree, but brown rot is by far the commonest and the concentric rings of pustules are characteristic. Sometimes, when trees are laden with a heavy crop and the fruit hang close to bare earth, other disease-causing organisms may be splashed on to them after heavy rain.

Cultural treatment Nothing can be done to eliminate totally the risk of brown rot attack, especially on large trees. The decay usually begins, however, at the point where fruit have been damaged (by birds or insect pests for instance) and its effects can be kept to a minimum therefore by taking all possible precautions to limit this type of wounding. Take especial care with fruit needed for storage: reject those with any signs of damage, handle carefully to minimise bruising, never pull out the stalk, and check the store regularly, being sure to remove promptly any fruit showing signs of decay (see page 52). Where rot of other types is a problem on low-hanging fruit, the damage can be minimised by grassing close to the trees or otherwise protecting the bare soil from the effects of rainfall.

Chemical treatment None really worthwhile in gardens.

Resistant varieties None.

Pear leaf blister mite

Although attacks of this common pest usually result only in yellowish leaf blisters that gradually darken as the season progresses, it may, on occasions, cause more serious damage with distortion of the shoots and consequent effects on the trees' vigour. As with most species of mite, control is difficult for few chemicals are effective and the only really helpful procedure is to collect up and burn the affected leaves. A spray with benomyl, better known as a fungicide, may be of some value but don't expect it to control the mites completely.

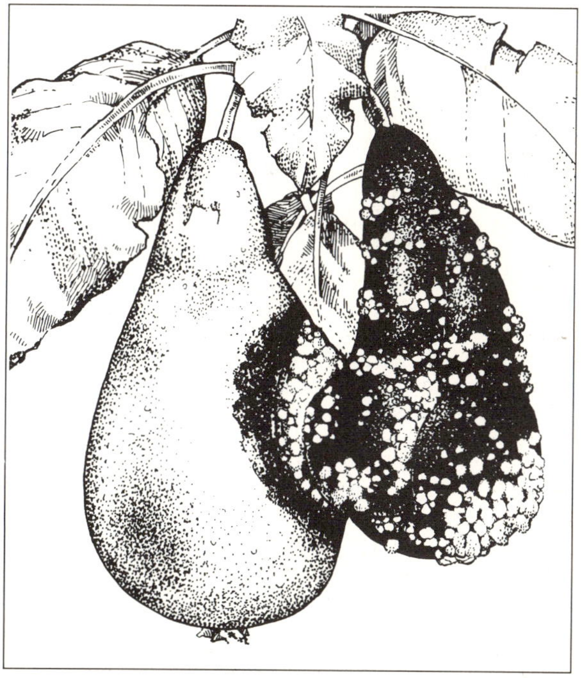

Silver leaf

Affects plums, apples, cherries and many other types of tree and shrub although it is always most serious on plums, especially Victoria.
Recognition The most distinctive feature, which gives the disease its name, is a silvery sheen to the foliage which results from the leaf tissues separating and allowing air to enter between them. The wood of affected branches has a brown stain within, and gradually twigs, branches and entire trees may die back. The bark may bear flat, purplish fungal growths but not always.
Possible confusion with false silver leaf. The silvery sheen to the leaves is distinctive, but it is not unique for similar symptoms can arise in a condition known as false silver leaf. This is a nutritional disorder indicating that the trees are short of fertiliser and, unlike silver leaf, it gives rise to no staining in the wood.
Cultural treatment Quite commonly, the most satisfactory treatment for silver leaf is the simplest of all; to do nothing! Trees sometimes recover from the disease. Obviously, any branches that have died will not revive and these should be cut off and burned. If the brown staining actually extends into the trunk, the portents are ominous, however and if suckers emerge with silvered leaves, the rootstock will be diseased and the entire tree should be destroyed. Collection and destruction of the affected leaves is pointless for they do not actually contain the causal fungus.
Chemical treatment None.
Resistant varieties Among plums, the most susceptible trees, no varieties are truly resistant although gages and damsons tend to be affected least severely. Among other fruit trees, pears generally do not suffer from the disease.

Replant disease or soil sickness

If old fruit trees are removed and replaced on more or less the same site with young stock, the new plants sometimes fail to establish or thrive. Gardeners will be familiar with a similar phenomenon in roses and it is due to an imperfectly understood problem known as replant disease. Unlike the general decline that may take place when a single type of vegetable is cropped repeatedly on the same land, replant disease has little to do with nutrient deficiencies and, indeed, the old stock, before their removal, may well have been growing quite reasonably. It appears that soil-inhabiting fungi are probably the cause; the older plants' root systems were able continuously to tap fresh, uncontaminated soil but the new plants, vulnerable because of the the transplanting shock, just find themselves unable to cope with the damage to their roots that infection causes. There is no cure; the treatment is to move the trees to a totally fresh site or to excavate and replace the soil. The former is usually the most satisfactory recourse with fruit trees although the latter works well with roses.

Plum rust

Affects plums and, to a lesser extent, peaches and almonds. Rust diseases are not found on apple or pear trees in gardens.
Recognition Bright yellow spots on the leaves which also bear dark brown or black dusty patches beneath. In severe attacks, the leaves wither and drop with consequent weakening of the trees.
Treatment On large trees, no control is really feasible but if the trees are young and/or growing on a dwarfing rootstock, it may be worthwhile spraying them with mancozeb; once when the fruit are half grown and again after they have been picked. Because the plum fungus can also affect anemones, it may be worth checking any in the garden for signs of disease on them as they could be the source of the problem.

Canker

Affects all types of fruit tree, but it is important to appreciate that the canker disease of apples and pears is quite different in cause, effect and treatment from that affecting plums and cherries. Many types of ornamental tree may be affected also and the comments below relating to apple and pear canker are equally applicable to them.
Recognition The typical form that canker disease takes is in the development of sunken, more or less circular or elongate 'target-like' lesions on the branches or, sometimes, the main stems. These lesions extend slightly and imperceptibly each season

until eventually they may totally girdle the stem which thus dies beyond that point. Plum and cherry canker is somewhat different in form with more or less irregular but extensive cratering of the bark and long, sunken depressions exuding quantities of gum. Commonly the leaves of affected trees are holed or tattered.
Possible confusion with mechanically caused wounds on trees (such as those lesions arising where branches have broken off, where the trunk has been struck forcibly or where wire has been tied around it). Such lesions tend to occur singly, unlike cankers which usually affect several parts of a tree, and, indeed, several different trees, simultaneously. Such mechanical wounds do not, of course, extend annually. The exuding of gum on plums and cherries is a common response to wounding of all kinds and only when it occurs very extensively is canker likely to be the cause.
Cultural treatment Whilst it cannot be pretended that good tree husbandry will remove totally the likelihood of canker development, certain precautions are sensible. Canker lesions must be cut out during the winter and burned; this is especially important where new trees are to be planted in a garden already containing diseased individuals. If the amount of cankering is severe, then the trees should be destroyed totally; but if the retention of old, cankered trees is necessary, it must be stressed that the planting of new stock nearby will be a waste of money. On plums and cherries, where the lesions are more diffuse and where the causal organism is likely to be present throughout the tissues of the tree and not confined to the obviously damaged areas, felling and uprooting is the only recourse. Take especial care when tying young cherry and plum trees to stakes for if the bark is abraded, this can facilitate entry of the pathogen.

Apple canker – a small lesion (actual size)

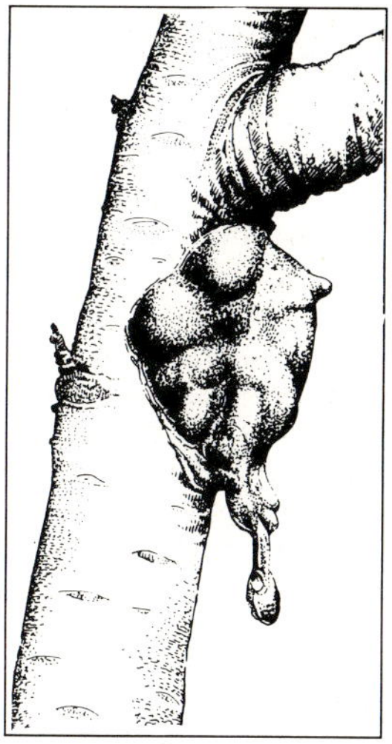

Plum canker exuding gum (enlarged)

Chemical treatment Because the fungus-causing apple and pear canker infects trees through the scars left by falling leaves in the autumn, a fungicide spray at that time is sometimes advocated to prevent infection. This is unlikely to make much difference to the likelihood of infection arising however; rigorous cutting out of any young lesions is much more important and valuable.
Resistant varieties All varieties of fruit trees are prone to cankering but if the garden or neighbourhood has a known history of the disease, then apple varieties such as Bramley's Seedling or Newton Wonder, which tend to be attacked less severely, are sensible choices.

Bigger pests of fruit

When pests attain the size of birds, not only does control become an emotional matter but the law steps in to afford them protection. The major problem bird among fruit crops is the bullfinch which moves into gardens in small flocks in the winter. Whilst soft fruit can be adequately protected with netting or with a more permanent fruit cage, it is almost impossible to protect tree fruits.

Mature fruit are pecked by several bird species which create a wound and spoil any chance of storing them. These fruit must be removed before they decay and affect other, healthy ones nearby.

Wasps commonly follow on the activities of birds and enlarge the initial peck wounds but if the damaged fruit are removed promptly, the numbers of insects will be diminished. Only if a wasp's nest is in, or very close to, dwellings where childen or persons with particularly severe allergic reactions to stings are likely to be attacked, is eradication with chemicals justified. It should never be forgotten that, for much of the year, wasps feed on other insects, many of which are much more serious pests than are the wasps themselves.

Bullfinches are a threat to fruit crops.

Peach leaf curl

Affects peaches, nectarines and, most seriously, almonds; but not, fortunately, either ornamental cherries or plums.
Recognition Shortly after the young leaves unfold in spring, they take on a puckered and crumpled appearance and soon become covered with a white powder. As the summer progresses, they gradually turn red then, finally, brown and shrivelled and may ultimately drop. If attacks develop repeatedly, the vigour of the tree will decline although its grossly disfiguring effect on plants that are often grown primarily as ornamentals is serious enough.
Possible confusion with the leaf-curling plum aphid. Although unlikely to be confused with other problems on peaches and almonds, similar leaf puckering can develp on plum trees as a result of infection by the leaf-curling plum aphid, which needs quite different treatment (see below).
Cultural treatment It is often imagined that destruction of affected leaves will eliminate the problem of leaf curl disease. This is only partly true (and, of course, only feasible on small trees). If the damaged leaves are collected from the tree during the early part of the season and burned, this will have some effect in diminishing the problem. Once the white 'bloom' has appeared however, it is really too late to make much impact for the spores of the leaf curl fungus will by then have been shed. It should also be appreciated that the fungus does not survive during the winter on the leaves at all; it persists on and among the bark and bud scales and thus it is to the leafless branches that chemical treatments should be applied.
Chemical treatment The best time to apply a spray is during the early spring, as the young buds are beginning to burst; a second spray, just after the leaves have dropped in the autumn is often thought to be beneficial also. The most effective chemical is Bordeaux Mixture but it must be appreciated that two or three years' treatment may be needed to master the problem on a badly affected tree.

Scab

Affects apples and pears especially. Scab is the term used for diseases that result in a hard, crusty patchiness. The scab disease of potatoes and root vegetables is a quite unrelated problem (see page 48).
Recognition Scab affects leaves, fruit and twigs, although twig symptoms are usually mistaken for tiny cankers. On the leaves, rounded, dark, dusty blotches form whilst on the fruit the characteristic scabby lesions develop.
Possible confusion with leaf spotting from various causes, but the combination of both fruit and foliar symptoms is diagnostic for scab.
Cultural treatment As the scab fungus survives mainly on the leaves during the winter, these should be collected up and burned after an attack has occurred. Twig lesions should also be cut out if they are found.
Chemical treatment Timing is important with spray treatments; they should be applied every two weeks from the time of bud burst until blossom fall, unless the disease is very severe, when the sprays need to be continued throughout the season. Benomyl or thiophanate-methyl are the best chemicals to use.

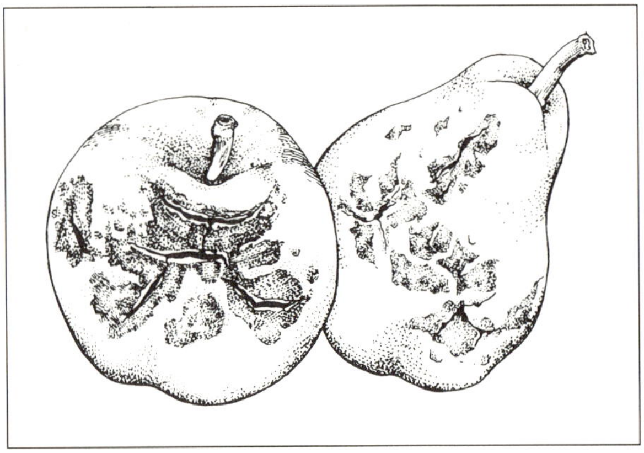

Scab on apple and pear

General The question is often asked whether apples and pears affected with scab are safe to eat. The answer is yes! Sometimes they even seem to be sweeter than normal but this is no justification for not controlling the disease!

Aphids

Affect all fruit trees, although the most conspicuous damage is probably that on plums caused by the leaf-curling aphid. In many years, some of the inevitable minor infestations may be tolerated without the need for treatment.
Recognition Usually, the first sign of aphid infestation is the appearance on the leaves of sticky honeydew excreted by the insects but, on close inspection, the green, grey, black, brown or yellow creatures themselves will be seen. Depending on the aphid species involved, there may be curling of the leaves and distortion of the shoots and, on plums, this can reach quite dramatic proportions with the twisted and crumpled leaves covered in honeydew, black sooty mould growth and the discarded skins of aphids. A rather different effect on apple trees is brought about by attacks of the woolly aphid which induces swelling and cracking of the bark on twigs and branches and which forms small colonies covered in a waxy, white 'wool'.
Possible confusion with apple canker and peach leaf curl. The invariable presence of the insects is diagnostic but the secondary effects of the woolly aphid may be confused with the symptoms of apple canker,

whereas the curling induced by the leaf-curling plum aphid is sometimes confused with that brought about by peach leaf curl disease although this does not, in fact, affect plum trees.
Cultural treatment None, except insofar as cutting out branches badly infested with the woolly aphid is a sound practice.
Chemical treatment Fortunately, aphids may be controlled relatively easily with any of a wide range of garden insecticides but it must be appreciated that large, old trees cannot realistically be treated. Although gardeners may find tar oil winter washes to be laborious and tedious to apply, there is no doubt that they do reduce the numbers of eggs and insects overwintering on the bark. Care is needed with this chemical nonetheless – keep eyes and skin well-protected and lay plastic or other sheeting to cover grass or other vegetation beneath the trees. Only apply tar oil when the trees are quite dormant (December is the best month).

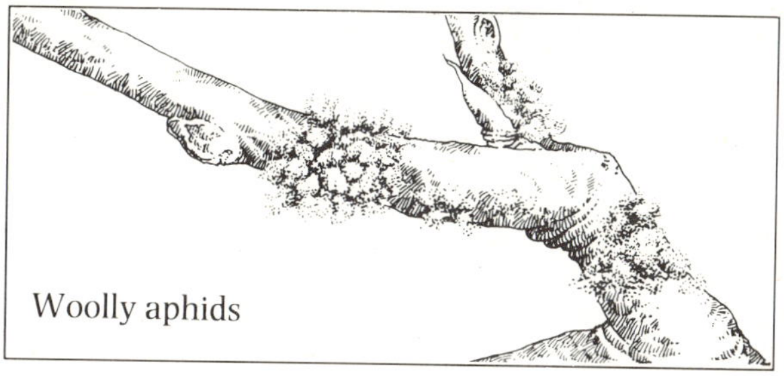
Woolly aphids

Also spray trees thoroughly, if possible, just before and after flowering, preferably with a modern systemic insecticide such as dimethoate.

Pest-damaged apples

Three types of pest damage are exceedingly common on apples and although two of the pests are usually found in the act of devouring the ripe fruit, the other leaves only characteristic malformations to betray its activites. The number one pest is the codling moth, followed closely by the apple sawfly with the seldom seen capsid bug third.
Recognition Attack by the codling moth larvae is usually undetectable externally for the small caterpillars normally burrow into the fruit through the eye and are only discovered, together with the mangled tissues around them, when the apple is cut in half or bitten through. The larvae of the sawfly also tunnel into the fruit but, unlike the codling moth, they can often be detected externally for they usually cause a characteristic, curved, surface scarring. Capsid bugs are rarely seen but they leave typical bumps on the surface of the fruit and, quite commonly, tattered leaves also. The latter symptom is also seen when capsid bugs attack soft fruit, especially currant bushes.
Possible confusion with other pests and some physical factors which may cause malformations that may resemble the surface damage by capsids and sawflies; but the internal damage by both sawflies and codling moth is quite distinctive.
Cultural treatment The traditional protective treatment against the codling moth is to tie sacking around the trunks of trees in early summer with the objective of inducing the caterpillars to pupate underneath it. The sacking is later removed and the insects destroyed. Unfortunately, the practice is of dubious value for the damage to the current year's fruit will already have been done and, the following year, female moths can easily fly in from neighbouring trees to lay their eggs.
Chemical treatment Capsid bugs are too erratic in their occurrence and insufficiently serious in their effects to warrant chemical control measures. Protective treatment to control sawfly and, more especially, codling moth, is well worthwhile however, provided that the trees are small enough to make this a practical proposition. Spray with dimethoate or permethrin just after the petals have dropped, again when the fruitlets are the size of a small finger-nail and again about ten days later.

Powdery mildew

Affects almost all types of fruit tree, but it is consistently most serious on apples and few seasons pass without attacks being experienced in most gardens.
Recognition The dusty white covering to leaves, shoots and other parts of the tree is familiar and unmistakable. On peaches, the symptoms quite commonly spread to the young fruit also. Mildew infection may result in the blossom wilting and the leaves falling prematurely; a characteristic effect on apples is the shedding of all except the terminal tuft of leaves at the end of diseased shoots.
Possible confusion with peach leaf curl which also causes powdery white growth; the puckering of the leaves, however, is quite unlike the effects of mildew.
Cultural treatment It may be possible to check outbreaks of mildew by removing the affected leaves and shoots as soon as they are seen in spring. Obviously, this is only possible on very small trees and should be done carefully, without showering the white spores onto the unaffected leaves. On apples and pears, shoots affected in the previous season should also be cut out during the winter and burned.
Chemical treatment Even when the above routines have been followed, chemical treatment will usually be needed and is especially sensible in a season following a severe outbreak. Nonetheless, it must be accepted that large, old trees are not amenable to treatment and the ease with which small trees can be sprayed is one good reason for making new plantings with a dwarf or semi-dwarfing rootstock. Spray with benomyl or thiophanate-methyl at the early pink bud stage and repeat fortnightly until mid-July.

11. Soft Fruit

The various plants grown for soft fruit production in gardens belong to two distinct families – strawberries, raspberries, blackberries and hybrid berries in one, and currants and gooseberries in the other. As a consequence, they tend to suffer from a different range of problems, although some, such as mildew and aphids are common to them all. As with tree fruits, the importance of starting with healthy stock cannot be over-stressed and, indeed, as soft fruit have a much shorter life span, most gardeners are likely to make a soft fruit planting every few years, although some may go for a lifetime and never need to plant new fruit trees.

Big bud

Affects blackcurrants.
Recognition The problem known as 'big bud' is accurately named; some of the buds swell to an abnormal size early in the year and fail to open satisfactorily. This is only part of the story however, for the bud-swelling is brought about by an infestation of minute creatures known as gall mites. The secondary effects of gall mite attack are more insidious for they usually inject a virus into the plants which results in a gradual decline in vigour and diminution of fruiting. This condition, known as reversion, manifests itself gradually over a few seasons but if a severe outbreak of big bud is seen, the chances are that reversion is present also.
Cultural treatment Remove and burn the affected buds promptly. If the attack is relatively slight, it may be possible to eradicate an infestation in this way. Once a large number of buds regularly show the symptoms however and the quantity and quality of fruit production declines, uprooting and burning the bushes is the only sensible action. Always obtain the best quality planting stock from a reputable supplier and plant as far as possible from the site of diseased bushes. It makes sound sense to renew blackcurrant bushes every seven or eight years as a routine.
Chemical treatment There is no chemical treatment for reversion but a slight attack of big bud can sometimes be checked by spraying the bushes with benomyl after the infested buds have been removed and destroyed.

Rust

Among soft fruits, rust is seen most frequently on gooseberries and on blackberries, although on neither is it one of the commonest diseases. The symptoms on the two types of plant are rather different moreover; on gooseberries, orange-red pustules form on leaves and shoots and tiny, crater or pock-like bodies form on them during the summer. The leaves become curled and puckered. On blackberries and loganberries, reddish purple spots form on the leaves with yellow pustules beneath and yellow-orange, slit-like lesions on the canes. Damaged leaves and shoots should be cut out and burned and a protective spray of Bordeaux Mixture applied the following year as the young leaves unfold and again just before the flowers open.

Caterpillars and similar pests

Although most types of plant will be attacked by caterpillars at certain times, strawberries seem to escape much of their attention and, in the soft fruit garden, gooseberries, currants and, in some areas, raspberries are more likely to be attacked. The principal pest, by far, is the conspicuous black, yellow and white caterpillar of the magpie moth which can strip gooseberry and currant bushes bare of leaves. The green larvae of another insect pest known as the gooseberry sawfly can cause similar damage and responds to similar treatment – a spray with a contact insecticide such as permethrin as soon as the first symptoms are seen.

The caterpillars of the raspberry moth cause rather different damage; the tiny pink larvae tunnel into the young shoots causing them to wither and die. It is best combatted by paying careful attention to crop hygiene, the removal of damaged leaves and the routine pruning out of old canes each season.

Magpie moth caterpillar

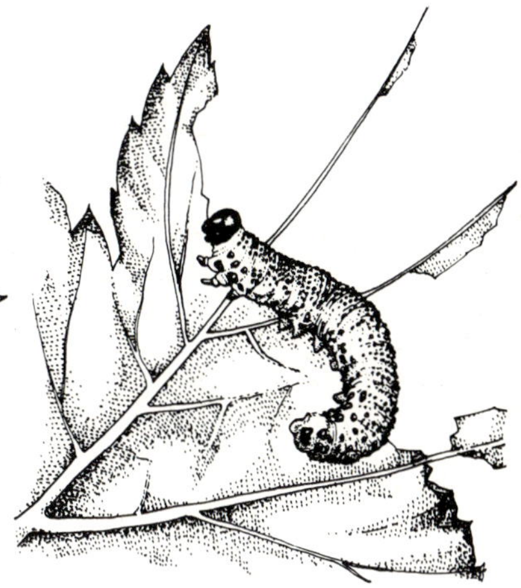
Gooseberry sawfly caterpillar

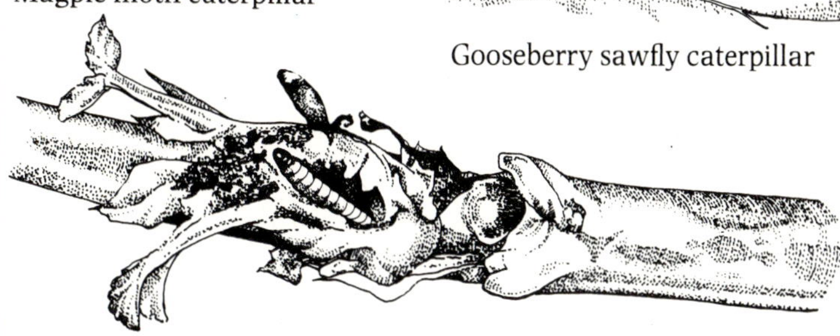
Raspberry moth caterpillar

Raspberry beetle

This is one of those garden pests that becomes apparent too late – when the fruit are being prepared or just as one is being popped into the mouth! The small, brownish grubs burrow into the ripening fruit and it is essential, therefore, that insecticide sprays (fenitrothion is the most effective) are applied immediately after the petals have fallen and before the insects have penetrated.

Leaf spots

Affect most types of soft fruit. In many instances the problem is not serious, and it is important, therefore, to be able to identify the potentially damaging forms.

Recognition On currants and gooseberries, small brown angular spots occur commonly and are often followed by premature dropping of the leaves. On strawberries, variously sized brown or purple spots are very common although rarely accompanied by significant damage. On raspberries and related berries, purple spots may develop on both leaves and canes with consequent distortion of the canes and loss of fruit.

Cultural treatment Affected leaves should be collected and burned, as far as this is practicable. Damaged rasberry canes should similarly be destroyed.

Chemical treatment After an attack has occurred, spray currants or gooseberries in the following season with benomyl or thiophanate-methyl immediately after flowering and again two weeks later. Raspberries should be sprayed at the time of bud burst and again two weeks later. There are no satisfactory chemical treatments for leaf spotting on strawberries but, by and large, this is a problem that gardeners need not be concerned with.

Resistant varieties None can be reliably recommended but the old raspberry varieties 'Lloyd George' and 'Norfolk Giant', the strawberries 'Cambridge Favourite' and 'Redgauntlet' and the redcurrants 'Fay's Prolific' and 'Fertility' are particularly prone to damage from leaf-spotting diseases. There are many modern varieties that are much more satisfactory.

Grey mould

The grey mould, *Botrytis*, appears in almost every plant section in the book for it is *the* ubiquitous pathogen, attacking and growing on all moribund or weakened plants, or the most soft and vulnerable of their tissues under damp, cool conditions. It affects all forms of soft fruit and is especially serious as a cause of fruit decay on strawberries, raspberries, blackberries and related hybrid berries such as boysenberries, loganberries and tayberries. On gooseberries, it is commonly more of a problem as a cause of dying back of the shoots.

The powdery grey mould is familiar to all gardeners and is unlikely to be confused with any other problem. The powdery growth of mildew is white, not grey, and tends to affect the parts of the plant on which grey mould is generally less severe – the leaves and shoots.

Certain measures will help minimise the effects of grey mould. Bush and cane fruits should be adequately spaced and carefully pruned to avoid overcrowding and strawberries should be mulched with bracken or straw as the fruit ripen to minimise contact with the soil. Nonetheless, ultimately, the likelihood of attacks developing is in the lap of the weather and some chemical protection is therefore wise. The most reliable chemicals for grey mould control are benomyl and thiophanate-methyl, both of which will effect some eradication of the disease if applied immediately after the symptoms appear. Better, however, is a protective spray before damage occurs and, as the initial infection normally arises through the flowers, not directly onto the fruit, the chemical should be applied shortly after the flowers open, with a repeat treatment about ten days later.

Mildew

Affects all soft fruits to some degree but the symptoms on strawberries are rather different from those on currants and gooseberries. Raspberries are not usually affected to any significant extent.

Recognition On strawberries, the leaves tend to curl up at the edges before turning brown – symptoms that are often confused with the effects of water shortage. Turning the leaves over will usually reveal at least a small amount of whitish mildew growth. The effects on raspberries, when they occur, are somewhat similar. On currants and, more seriously, gooseberries, a typical white powdery covering forms on the leaves and young shoots, followed later in the season by a brown, felty growth.

Treatment Always take care to prune bushes regularly to maintain a good air circulation. Avoid any excessive use of nitrogen-rich fertilizers and never plant soft fruit in a shady part of the garden. Affected strawberry foliage should be burned off at the end of the season. Chemical treatment may be necessary in dry years and the best to use are benomyl or thiophanate-methyl. Spray gooseberries as the flowers open, repeat after fruit set and again two weeks later. Currants should be sprayed as the flowers open and again every two weeks until early July. Sulphur is sometimes recommended for strawberry mildew but can damage some varieties and is better avoided. Benomyl or thiophanate-methyl are more reliable and can be applied as frequently as fortnightly after the first signs of disease are seen.

Red spider mite

Affects strawberries – this is the crop most likely to be affected among soft fruit but red spider mites also infest a wide range of other plants, especially in greenhouses and houses (see page 13).

Recognition Red spider mites are exceedingly small (about 0.5 mm in length) and the first indications of an attack are usually a speckling, discolouration and withering of the leaves. On close inspection, the affected plants will be seen to be festooned with a cobweb-like coat, while closer inspection still may reveal the tiny creatures themselves, crawling over the webs.

Treatment As with all species of mite, treatment is not easy for very few insecticides affect them and physical eradication is difficult because of their small size. The most useful advice therefore is to try to capitalise on the mites' dislike of damp conditions – attacks are always worse in hot, dry seasons. Regular watering, the use of mulches and the mist-spraying of the strawberry bed during warm and sunny weather are especially important. The misting should be applied at least twice daily if infested plants are found but once the attack gains a major hold, it is unlikely

that the damage can be arrested and it is wise to uproot and burn the stock and start afresh the following seaason.
General Rather larger, bright red coloured mites may often be seen scurrying along garden paths and in sheds or greenhouses. These are not a cause for panic however; they are not red spider mites and some actually prey on the pest species.

Problems affecting raspberry canes

Although raspberry canes may bear the lesions associated with leaf spotting diseases (p. 33), there is a group of other, specifically cane problems that are partially interrelated and can cause quite serious damage. The three problems making up this group are cane midge, cane blight and spur blight.
Recognition Cracking of the bark is the most obvious symptom of cane midge attack and, during summer and autumn, small pinkish maggots may be discovered, feeding within these cracks. Very commonly, such damage is followed by infection with the fungus causing cane blight disease, in which blackened areas spread outwards from the cracks with consequent shrivelling of the leaves and general dying back and debilitation of the canes. Spur blight tends to be a problem of more northern areas and, like cane blight, may follow attack by the cane midge. Lengths of cane turn brown and the buds on affected parts die, resulting in a loss of fruiting capacity. In winter, these cane lesions take on a characteristic silvery colour.

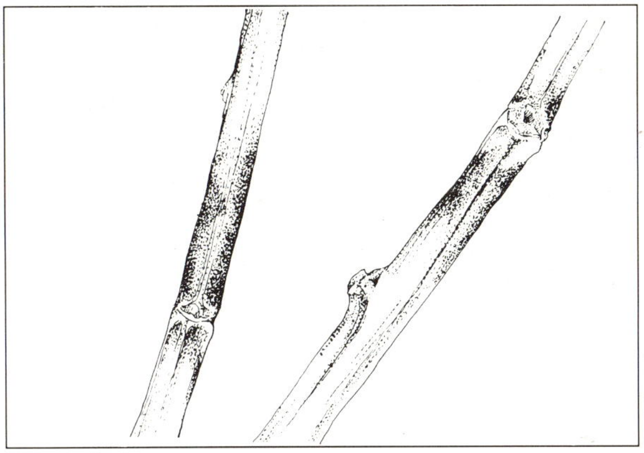

The effect on raspberry canes of midge attack

Cultural treatment Any damaged canes should be cut out and burned and attention paid to general husbandry, removing all old canes and thinning out new ones as appropriate for the variety.
Chemical treatment A routine spray with fenitrothion in early May, repeated about two weeks later, will minimise the likelihood of cane midge attack. The routine early-season spraying with benomyl or thiophanate-methyl to prevent grey mould infection should help to protect the plants against cane and spur blight also. These fungicides should also be used following the removal of damaged canes.
Resistant varieties 'Malling Admiral' and 'Leo' have some resistance to spur blight. Conversely, 'Malling Jewel' and 'Malling Promise' are particularly prone to midge attack.

Viruses

In addition to the rather special case of reversion disease on blackcurrants (page 32), other types of soft fruit are also prone to virus contamination. In most instances, the symptoms are well-evident. On raspberries and blackberries, an irregular pattern of pale green or yellowish areas develops on the leaves (not to be confused with the very common and more uniform inter-veinal yellowing that arises on alkaline soils and may be corrected by the application of sequestered iron); on blackberries, a pronounced stunting may occur with few fruit forming and weak and short canes being produced; on gooseberries and currants, a pale yellow colour may develop on and around the leaf veins, whilst on strawberries, various forms of stunting, leaf malformation and irregular yellowing may occur with, occasionally, the development of small, green flowers.

The likelihood of most of the above problems arising may be minimised by careful attention to aphid control throughout the season for these are the commonest means of virus being introduced into the stock. Once the symptoms develop severely however, it is wise to uproot and burn the plants, replanting if at all possible, on a fresh site. It is essential that new stock be obtained from a reputable supplier and is stated to be 'certified'. This will guarantee that it has been produced in a manner to ensure that it is free from virus contamination at the time of purchase.

Aphids

As with almost every other species of garden plant, aphids of varying colours may infest all types of soft fruit, resulting in distorted leaves and shoots and possibly introducing virus contamination. Routine protection should be given therefore with almost any of the modern garden insecticide sprays, although care should be taken to follow the manufacturers' directions not to spray when the plants are flowering, as bees and other pollinating insects may be killed, and to be especially careful with strawberries under polythene or glass which are readily damaged by some chemicals.

12. Vegetable Fruit

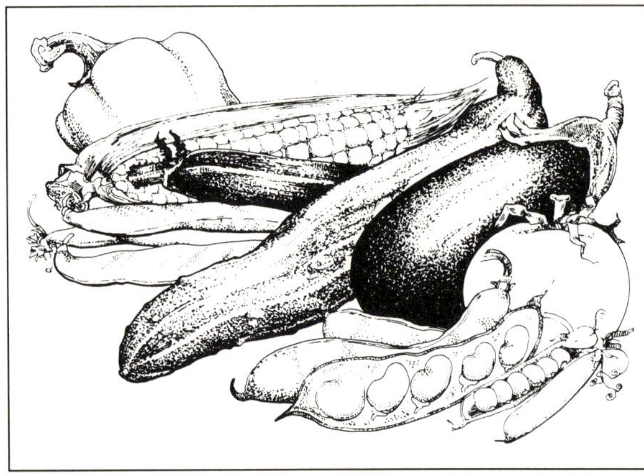

Vegetable fruits are those crops that are classified and grown as vegetables but which are cultivated for their fruit, not the leafy, vegetative growth or flowers. They include both greenhouse and outdoor tomatoes, cucumbers, marrows, courgettes and pumpkins, pepper and egg plants as well as peas, beans and sweet corn. Most of the common problems associated with these crops are described here; the only major problem not considered is the red spider mite, which can be very damaging and is described on page 34.

Leaf mould

Affects tomatoes in greenhouses; infrequently, outdoor plants also.
Recognition Yellowing patches on the leaves with a brown or greyish mould beneath which may spread to affect entire leaves. If conditions are sufficiently moist, the foliage may drop and fruit production suffer as a result.
Possible confusion with botrytis grey mould and potato blight (page 48); these may affect tomato leaves but the latter is commoner on outdoor than greenhouse plants and neither display the brownish growth that is especially characteristic of leaf mould.
Cultural treatment Good ventilation is the key to avoiding leaf mould infection – warm, humid and stagnant air in greenhouses must be avoided and the value of vents low down in the sides cannot be overstressed in this regard.
Chemical treatment If ventilation is provided, routine protective spraying against leaf mould should not be necessary. Nonetheless, if attacks can be detected sufficiently early, sprays at fortnightly intervals with mancozeb, benomyl or thiophanate-methyl should check the disease. Fruit should not be picked for three days after the application of chemical. If a severe outbreak has occurred, then the greenhouse should be fumigated with sulphur candles, but this must be done before the remains of the diseased crop are removed.

Botrytis grey mould

Affects all of the vegetable fruits if conditions are cool and damp; especially at flowering time, for the grey mould fungus commonly infects the developing fruit through the flowers.
Recognition The fruits of tomatoes, egg plants, cucumbers and marrows and the pods of peas and beans all display the familiar fluffy dark grey patches of mould, usually at the blossom end.
Possible confusion with other causes of decay – although grey mould is the commonest, it is not the only disease bringing about fruit decay. Among others are potato blight, which can affect tomatoes (page 48), blossom end rot (page 41) (not strictly a disease at all), and soft rot (page 49). Rot is frequent on outdoor crops whose fruit or pods hang close to the soil and become diseased when contaminated soil is splashed onto them; these are best checked by covering the soil with a suitable mulch of straw or other material. The chemical treatments recommended below for grey mould will be much less effective against other types of rot, and specific chemical treatments for many of them are not available. The cultural procedures will certainly help, however.
Cultural treatment It cannot be said too often that the control of grey mould means scrupulous attention to hygiene. Old plant debris must be cleared away promptly; dead or yellowed leaves should be removed

from the lower parts of tomato stems and any affected fruit destroyed.
Chemical treatment Benomyl or thiophanate-methyl are the best fungicides to use and are particularly valuable because they may control other diseases on the same plants. Spray at the first sign of symptoms and repeat two weeks later.
General In some parts of the country, strains of the grey mould fungus exist which are resistant to the effects of the fungicides suggested. Unfortunately, there is no longer a reliable alternative treatment for gardeners to use but it should be pointed out that excessive use of benomyl or thiophanate-methyl may increase the likelihood of more resistant strains developing. Use them in moderation therefore.

Ghost spot

Affects tomatoes, either in unheated greenhouses or outdoors, especially as the weather cools towards the end of the season.
Recognition Small, off-white, circular spots or rings on the fruit.
Possible confusion with lime deposits. In hard water areas, a lime deposit may form on the fruit if tap water is splashed onto them and allowed to dry. Unlike ghost spot, this can be wiped off.
Treatment As ghost spot more often causes concern than damage, direct action is rarely called for. It is, however, a mild symptom of attack by botrytis grey mould and the routine preventatives outlined above will help limit its occurrence.

Aphids

Affect all vegetable fruit crops, both in greenhouses and outdoors. In greenhouses, tomatoes, cucumbers, peppers and egg-plants are also likely to be affected by the consequent growth of sooty moulds on the honeydew secreted by the insects. Outdoors, broad beans are most commonly and most severely affected.
Recognition There can be few gardeners who are unable to recognise aphids. In greenhouses, the commonest species are the archetypal 'greenfly' in varying shades of green. Whilst the same or related species will also be found out-doors, the black species, known, naturally enough, as 'blackfly' is probably the most serious pest, causing severe stunting of young broad bean shoots.
Possible confusion with nothing else, although the sooty mould growth that follows aphid infestation can also arise after whitefly attack.
Cultural treatment There are a number of traditional remedies that are claimed to keep away aphids (see page 59) but one of the few basic treatments that really has much merit is the hose-pipe! A powerful jet of water will certainly remove aphids from broad bean plants, but it is rather chancy with more flimsy types of plant and is certainly inadvisable in the greenhouse. Pinching out the young infested

shoots early in the season can also be very effective.
Chemical treatment Fortunately, aphids may be controlled quite easily with almost any of the general garden insecticides.

Whitefly

Affect equally all the vegetable fruit crops in greenhouses; generally much less of a problem outdoors.
Recognition Clouds of small white, moth-like insects fly up when plants are disturbed – as they tend to congregate on the undersides of the leaves, their presence is often not appreciated until the foliage is moved. As with aphid attack, the secondary effects of sooty mould growth are frequently more significant than the direct damage caused by the insects.
Cultural treatment From time to time, publicity is given to a method of biological control of whitefly in greenhouses by the introduction of a small species of parasitic wasp called *Encarsia* which lays its eggs on the immature whiteflies. Advertisements will be seen for small 'starter' cultures of the wasp. Unfortunately, such biological control, though excellent in principle, is rarely successful on a small scale and it suffers from the disadvantage that the insecticides needed to control other greenhouse pests cannot be used because they would adversely affect the parasite.
Chemical treatment Whitefly control with chemicals is difficult although not impossible. Because the adult insects are fairly susceptible to such products as permethrin or dimethoate, whereas the immature forms are not, the keys to successful control are vigilance and repeat treatments every two or three weeks. Especial care must be taken to spray non-systemic materials, like permethrin, thoroughly on the undersides of the leaves.

Pea moth

Affects only peas.
Recognition The pea moth caterpillars are usually not apparent until it is too late – when the pods are being shelled in the kitchen and the tiny yellowish-white larvae poke out their little black heads from holes in the peas and the pods are seen to be filled with a mass of chewed fragments. There is no damage to the leaves.
Cultural treatment Pea moth control is not easy with chemicals and the available cultural methods should be considered seriously: the principle is to try and ensure that the flowers and young pods are not present when the female pea moths are laying their eggs early in July. Choose carefully therefore those varieties which do not need to be sown in March and April; sow either earlier or later.
Chemical treatment Even if the sowing time is chosen carefully, and even though chemicals are not always entirely satisfactory, a spray with permethrin a few days after the first flowers appear, and again about two weeks later, makes sound sense.
Resistant varieties None; don't believe any claims that you may see to the contrary.

Spots on beans

Affect broad, dwarf and runner beans in different forms.
Recognition The spotting varies: on broad beans, chocolate spot is the commonest symptoms with rich brown lesions that spread rapidly, darken and eventually result in much of the plant being blackened and shrivelled. On dwarf and runner beans, especially in wet seasons, a red colour to the leaf veins on the undersides of the leaves and reddish spots on the pods are the signs of anthracnose disease, whereas more or less circular spots with pronounced yellow halos on the leaves and pods are the symptoms of halo blight. The small, powdery pustules of bean rust may also sometimes be found on dwarf and runner beans.
Cultural treatment Chocolate spot can be minimised by not sowing broad beans too closely together, by not planting in any degree of shade, by not planting on waterlogged soils and by not applying nitrogenous fertilisers. Anthracnose and rust can scarcely be avoided in this way, but the likelihood of halo blight attack can be lessened by not soaking seeds in water before planting (this transfers the bacteria responsible for the problem from one seed to another); pack them over-night in damp peat instead, if you wish to start them in this way.
Chemical treatment Benomyl or thiophanate-methyl, sprayed fortnightly, may go some way towards checking chocolate spot, while zineb may similarly arrest rust development.
Resistant varieties There appears to be little effective resistance available to chocolate spot, bean rust, or halo blight whereas many varieties of dwarf bean are resistant to anthracnose and may be so indicated in catalogues.

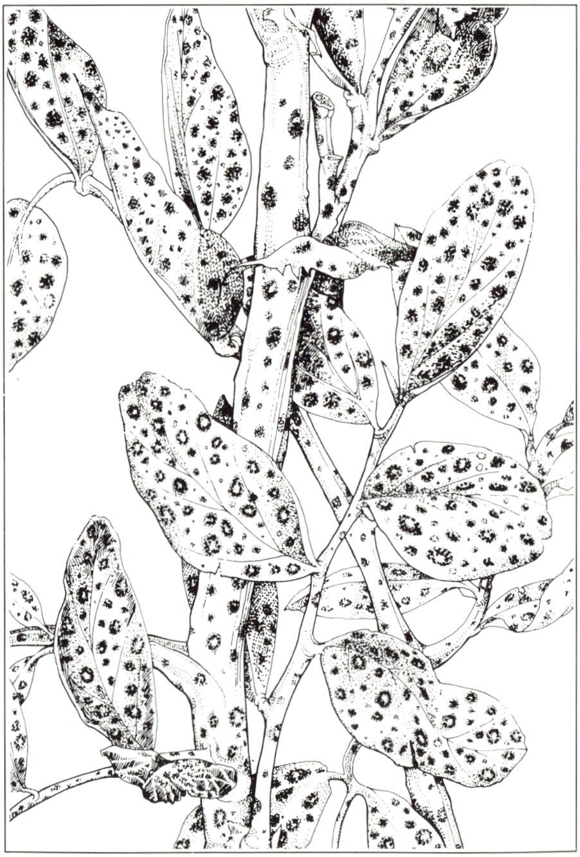

Chocolate spot on broad beans

Sweet corn smut

This is one of the problems that gardeners, even those who grow sweet corn regularly, may not see for many years. When it does strike however, as it is likely to do in very hot and dry summers, the effects are quite unforgettable; the young cobs develop in a grotesque and distorted fashion and the seeds 'explode' to spill out a black sooty mass. Regrettably, once the disease strikes, there is really nothing that can be done to save the crop and the plants should be destroyed. Although the spores of the smut fungus seem to be widespread in the soil, it makes sound sense not to plant a new crop on the site where a previous crop has succumbed to the disease.

Root nodules

Any distortion on plant roots is likely to be spotted by the eagle-eyed gardener when he is transplanting or removing crop debris at the end of the season. More often than not, as a perusal of this book will verify, the cause is likely to be a pest or pathogen that has attacked or infected the root tissues and brought about abnormal growth: clubroot, cyst eelworm and turnip gall weevil are good examples. When peas, beans and other members of the pea family such as sweet peas, lupins and cytisus are uprooted, the discovery of small, knobbly swellings is a cause for satisfaction, not despondency. The swellings are known as root nodules and they are formed by certain types of bacteria that live within the root tissues. These bacteria have the unusual attribute of being able to convert nitrogen gas from the air into a form that plants can utilise; thus they enhance the nitrogen fertiliser status of the soil. For this reason, nitrogenous fertilisers should not be applied to plants of the pea family (or, at least, should only be applied in small quantities) because excessive lush, leafy growth will result. The added nitrogen that such plants leave behind in the soil means, moreover, that peas and beans should be followed in a rotation in the vegetable garden by plants, such as leafy brassicas, that have a special need for it.

The illustration shows pea, lupin and cytisus (broom) plants, with a root bearing the characteristic nodules.

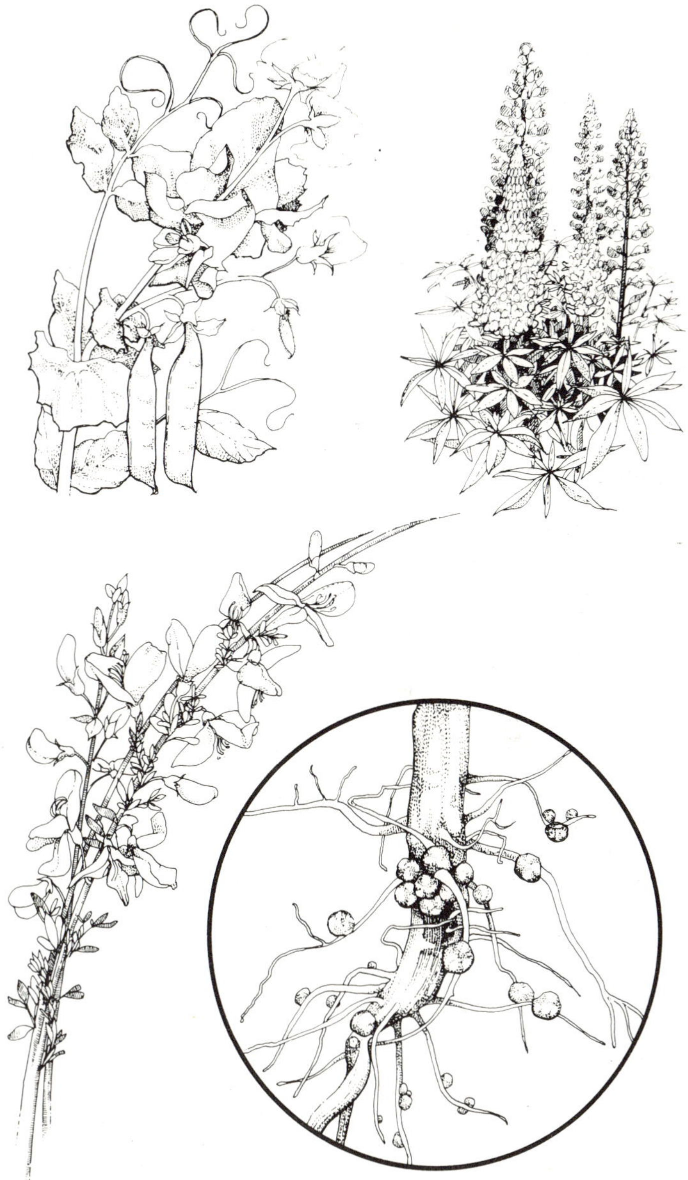

Leaf problems on tomatoes

Apart from the effects of leaf mould (page 36) and potato blight (page 48), which can give rise to mould growth on the leaves, tomato foliage very commonly displays other discolourations and malformations. Some of these are damaging, some not so, and it is important therefore that gardeners can recognise the symptoms. Here are the commonest, together with associated effects on other parts of the plants:

Symptom	*Probable cause*	*Treatment – comment*
Leaves, leaf stalks and stem, twisted, thickened and distorted.	Weedkiller damage	The usual source of the weedkiller is farmyard manure containing straw from treated cereal crops. In greenhouses, switch to growing bags; outdoors, rest the site for one season.
Leaves distorted and usually with yellowish blotches; fruit usually distorted also.	Virus	Destroy plants; do not save seed from them and raise the next season's crop on different land (outdoors) or in growing bags (greenhouse).
Leaves with rough, knobbly outgrowths on undersides.	Oedema	Improve greenhouse ventilation.
Leaves, especially those at the base of the plant, with pronounced yellowing between the veins.	Magnesium deficiency	Ensure balanced tomato feed is used.
Leaves curl and adopt a pronounced dark green colour.	Not a problem – a sign of good growth	None necessary.

Cucumber virus

Affects cucumbers. All kinds of vegetable fruit are affected by one or more types of virus. Generally, they are not important in gardens on peas and beans however, whilst virus problems on tomatoes are considered above. This leaves cucumbers and, to a lesser extent, marrows, courgettes and pumpkins which are all very commonly affected.

Recognition The leaves take on a crumpled or puckered appearance with irregular yellowish streaks and blotches. When the infection is severe, the plant as a whole is reduced in vigour. The fruit also become mis-shapen and have a bitter taste.

Possible confusion with pollinated fruit; the bitter tasting fruit should not be confused with the bitterness that develops in some cucumber varieties as a result of the female flowers having been allowed to become pollinated by the male flowers. Some fertiliser deficiencies may give rise to leaf yellowing, but distortion is the characteristic of virus.

Treatment Once a plant is showing signs of virus infection, there is nothing that can be done to save it and it really should be destroyed to prevent the disease from spreading. Even though many gardeners only grow one or two cucumber plants, and may feel they would prefer to keep them and make the most of any crop that is produced, it should be remembered that the problem will not only also affect marrows and courgettes, but the particular virus responsible for this problem can be spread to an enormous range of other types of garden plant too. The cucumber virus, in common with many other types of virus, is carried by aphids and routine control of these pests is vital to minimise the likelihood of infection becoming established.

Powdery mildew

Affects cucumbers, marrows, courgettes, pumpkins and also peas.

Recognition A dusty white covering to the leaves which soon become yellowed and wilt. As cucurbits have large, but relatively few leaves for the size of plant, the growth of mildew on them may quite rapidly have a serious impact on their overall growth and vigour. Curative treatments must be applied promptly therefore.

Possible confusion with several factors that can cause leaves to wilt, most notably a shortage of water in hot weather, but the powdery white growth is always diagnostic for mildew.

Cultural treatment In greenhouses, it should be possible to minimise the likelihood of mildew developing by ensuring adequate ventilation, although this makes it difficult to maintain the high humidity that cucumbers need.

Chemical treatment Spray promptly with thiophanate-methyl or benomyl and repeat two or three times at approximately ten-day intervals.

Resistant varieties 'Disease-resistance' is claimed in seed catalogues for several cucumber and/or marrow varieties; usually however, this refers to virus diseases and no garden varieties are reliably resistant to mildew.

Wilts and root rots

Affect tomatoes, peas and beans.
Recognition An overall yellowing and stunting, usually with some dropping of the leaves and with blackening at the stem base and on the roots indicates root rot. Wilts are superficially similar but the drooping of the foliage is usually more dramatic. If the stem is split open 8–12 ins (20–30 cm) above ground level, a brown staining will be apparent within if a wilt disease is responsible.
Possible confusion with any factor that damages roots or starves plants of water, thus causing the leaves to wilt, but the brown staining in the stem tissues is diagnostic.
Cultural treatment This is very difficult because the fungi responsible for root rots and wilts are almost impossible to eradicate from the soil. In the greenhouse, therefore, a switch to growing bags is the only effective way to avoid the problem. Outdoors, the resting of the soil for as long as possible from plants of the same type may enable the disease-causing fungi to die away. All other soil factors that might affect plant growth (fertilisers, drainage, pH and soil structure, for example) should also be attended to.
Chemical treatment Chemical control of root rots and wilts is very difficult but the use of a spray-strength solution of thiophanate-methyl or benomyl around affected plants as a drench, repeated at two-week intervals, is worth trying, especially if the crops are approaching maturity.
Resistant varieties Some tomato varieties have resistance to wilt and to some forms of root rot. It would be wise to use these, therefore, especially if space is limited outdoors and alternative land is not available. In greenhouses, the growing bag system is a far simpler solution.

Splitting, blackening and rotting

Two of the most common of all problems with tomatoes arise as a result of neither pest nor disease; both are related however to the availability to the plant of water and serve to emphasise how important a regular, steady water supply is to the tomato plant. If the plants have experienced a shortage of water when the fruit are ripening (such as might occur during a fairly long period of dry weather, or a gardener's holiday), and have then been watered steadily and liberally, the result is very often that the fruit will split. Some varieties are claimed to be less prone than others to such splitting but all are likely to be affected to some degree if they suffer a check in their water supply.

Split tomato

A shortage of water, such as can and does occur very commonly in growing bags which dry out unseen, may be followed by the development of hard, leathery patches on the developing fruit. This is generally known as blossom end rot and is due to a shortage in the fruits of the element calcium, a condition exacerbated when the plants are dry at the roots. Provided it is not too severe, blossom end rot, unlike splitting, can often be cured: the treatment is to spray the fruit (not the leaves) with a solution containing approximately 2g per litre of calcium nitrate; a chemist should be able to make this up.

Blossom end rot

Decay of tomato fruit follows fungal or bacterial infection. Mould growth may be present but is not inevitable; the hard, brownish lesions of blight, in particular, commonly have no mould on them (see page 48). Other common causes of decay are botrytis (page 36) and soft rot (page 49).

13. Leafy Vegetables

Included here are the problems likely to be found on lettuces, celery, spinach and all the leafy brassicas, including cabbages, cauliflowers and Brussels sprouts, although pests and diseases that have their principal effect on brassica roots will be found described in the section that covers turnips and swedes (page 46). As the leafy parts of these plants are the object of cultivation, less damage can be tolerated on the leaves than it can with most other garden plants.

Caterpillars on leaves

Affect most types of vegetables, but by far the most important caterpillars are the various butterfly and moth caterpillars on brassicas.
Recognition In severe attacks, the leaves are stripped to the veins and the caterpillars themselves will be readily apparent. Most important are the black and yellow caterpillars of the large white butterfly but the green larvae of the small white butterfly and the fat, green or brown ones of the cabbage moth can be equally damaging in some seasons. When attacks are less severe, characteristic holding of the leaves will be seen, with the plants fouled by droppings.
Possible confusion with nothing else.
Cultural treatment Nothing can be done to prevent butterflies from laying their eggs, but regular inspection of the crops should mean that the pests can be picked off by hand before they reach damaging levels. It may also be possible to spot the tiny yellow egg masses and remove these.
Chemical treatment Many people find collecting caterpillars by hand unpleasant and prefer a chemical treatment. There are many to choose from, but those containing the synthetic pyrethrum-like compounds, permethrin or resmethrin are probably the simplest and safest to use as crops can be harvested soon after treatment.

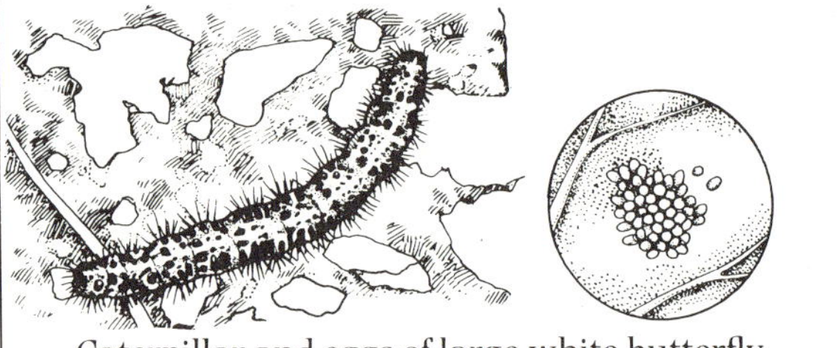
Caterpillar and eggs of large white butterfly

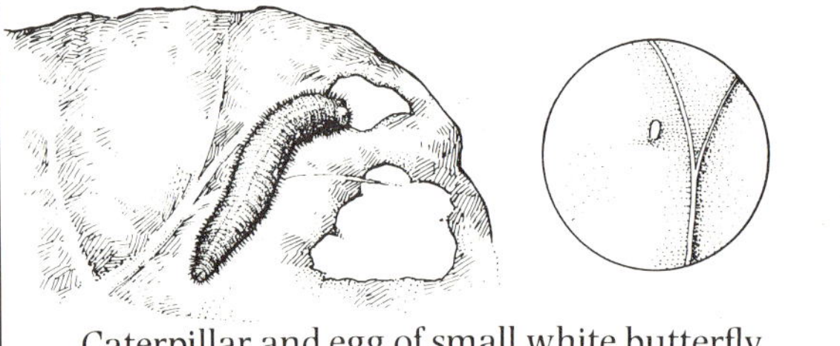
Caterpillar and egg of small white butterfly

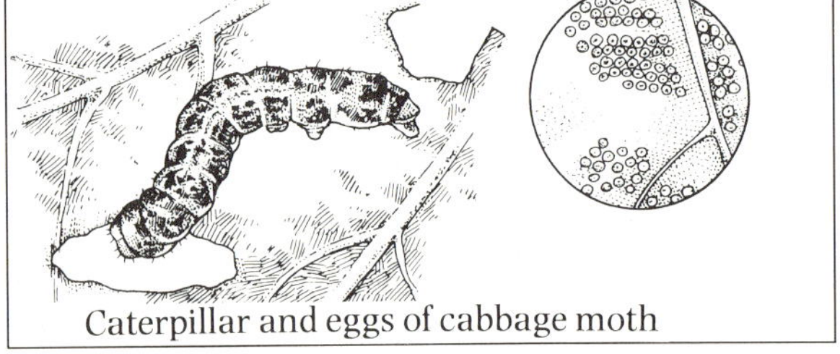
Caterpillar and eggs of cabbage moth

Leaf spots

Affect all leafy crops – each has its own leaf spot diseases but relatively few are serious.
Recognition The term leaf spot is self-explanatory but the actual lesions can vary greatly in size, shape and colour. The only ones that need concern gardeners are dark spots on cabbages or other brassicas, if present in large numbers; pale coloured spots with holes in the centre that sometimes arise on winter lettuce in cold, wet seasons; and masses of tiny brown spots on celery leaves.
Possible confusion with downy mildew (below), which produces angular lesions on brassica leaves but, in damp conditions, these bear an off-white mould growth on the undersides; slugs can cause holing but slime trails are usually present. Virus infection may also cause black spotting – see page 44.
Cultural treatment All crop debris must be cleared away at the end of the season for spot-forming fungi can survive on it over winter. As some fungi that cause leaf spot are carried on the seed, it is important, if possible, to buy fresh seed each season from a reputable supplier, rather than save your own; certainly, seed should never be saved from plants showing disease symptoms.
Chemical treatment It is scarcely worthwhile attempting to control many leaf spotting diseases, although celery leaf spot in particular may be usefully checked with one or two sprays of benomyl at fortnightly intervals. As aphid-carrying viruses may be responsible for some of the black spotting seen on brassica heads, routine aphid control is especially important (see next page).

Downy mildew

Affects brassicas, lettuces and, occasionally, spinach, although different fungi are responsible in each case and the disease cannot be transferred from one type of plant to the other. Downy mildew can also be responsible for a form of damping-off of brassica seedlings (see page 14).
Recognition Dirty yellow or brownish, characteristically angular spots develop on the upper leaf surfaces and gradually spread, causing large areas of leaf to die. There is usually an off-white mould growth on the underside of the lesions.
Possible confusion with leaf spots, which may be similar but they do not support mould growth and most types are less angular in appearance than the mildew lesions. Quite commonly, the grey mould fungus will attack leaf tissues damaged by downy mildew and thus hasten their decline.
Treatment In addition to the routine clearing away of crop debris, chemical controls may be tried; unfortunately however, the only treatment available for garden-use (sprays with mancozeb at fortnightly intervals up to two weeks before harvest) is not particularly effective.

Birds and rabbits

The birds that cause so much trouble among brassicas in more rural gardens, especially those close to farmland, tend to be different species from those damaging fruit (page 29) or seedlings (page 14). The leaf-eating wood pigeon is the most important although in some areas and in some seasons, a range of other types including partridges and collared doves may be troublesome. Rabbits are conveniently grouped with birds as they are large, voracious, appear in large numbers and are similarly difficult to control.

There are no easy answers to the problems of wood pigeons and rabbits; scaring devices, including modern audible or visual contraptions are generally no more effective than the traditional scarecrow, are far less attractive and often cause more disturbance to neighbours than to the pests. Shooting is scarcely practicable or legal in most gardens, whilst chemical repellents are of very limited effectiveness, most being readily washed away by rain. Ultimately, some form of physical barrier is needed in the shape of a small-mesh wire netting fence with a base buried at least 1 ft (30 cm) deep to keep out rabbits, or a net cover draped over supports to keep away pigeons.

Aphids

Affect all types of leafy vegetables but the cabbage aphid is particularly troublesome.
Recognition All gardeners will be familiar with the overall appearance of aphids, but the commonest of these on brassicas cannot be called greenfly or blackfly as their colour is predominantly grey. They occur in masses on the heads and among the leaves and although a heavy infestation can affect plant growth and vigour, it is more common for the damage to be discovered when, for example, a cauliflower reveals the aphids entrenched deep within its curd after it has been cooked and served on a plate.

A rather different type of aphid attack is that made by root aphids on lettuce plants, causing the plants to wilt; the white, root-infesting insects are apparent only when the affected plants are pulled up.

Cultural treatment Although some gardeners claim to be able to control aphid infestations by washing them off with a hose-pipe, this can scarcely be recommended as a viable treatment, especially on brassica heads where the insects are likely to reside in inaccessible nooks.
Chemical treatment The essential choice lies between quick-acting, but poorly penetrating chemicals such as permethrin and resmethrin, when only a short time is needed between spray and harvest, and the systemic chemicals such as dimethoate, which penetrate better but for which a longer interval must elapse before the crop may be eaten.
Resistant varieties None, except in the special case of lettuces and root aphids, where the varieties, Avoncrisp and Avondefiance are very reliable.

Botrytis grey mould

Affects all vegetables under damp and cool conditions if they are sufficiently stressed or weakened, but normally the most serious problems arise on lettuces; especially following attack by downy mildew.

Recognition The fluffy grey mould growth from which the disease takes its name is the most obvious symptom and covers the soft decomposing tissues of the leaves or head. Other rot-causing fungi and bacteria then tend to join forces with the botrytis so that the plant is soon reduced to a worthless mass. Sometimes, grey mould attacks the stems of lettuces, especially where they have been weakened by slugs or other pests and this results in the head falling over and shrivelling.

Possible confusion with other rotting diseases, although the grey mouldy growth is characteristic.

Cultural treatment Avoidance of primary causes of damage (downy mildew, slugs, inadequate fertiliser and over-watering, for example) will ensure that grey mould has little opportunity to infect.

Chemical treatment If the disease is persistently troublesome, and especially if the season is cool and damp, it would be wise to spray seedlings with benomyl or thiophanate-methyl and repeat the treatment every two to three weeks. This procedure is especially important with winter lettuce.

General Botrytis grey mould is probably the commonest of all garden diseases and will be found in every section of the book.

Powdery mildew

Affects brassicas.

Recognition One of the most familiar of all garden diseases; a velvety white coating appears over the leaves with consequent yellowing and general loss of vigour.

Possible confusion with downy mildew (page 43), but this is similar only in name, causing more discrete areas of dead tissue. A disease called white blister sometimes affects brassicas (especially cauliflowers and broccoli); it too causes discrete areas of whitish growth, but is almost always accompanied by severe distortion of the plant.

Cultural treatment Once more, the prompt clearing away of debris on which the mildew fungus might persist is most important.

Chemical treatment There is a wide range of effective mildew-controlling fungicides but some are only suitable for use on ornamental plants. On vegetable crops, thiophanate-methyl and benomyl are probably the most satisfactory treatments; the sprays may need to be repeated every two or three weeks, however, in hot dry summers.

General There are many different types of powdery mildew fungi and cross-infection between different types of plant is unusual; nonetheless, all require similar conditions and, therefore, a severe attack in the flower garden means that the problem may be expected on vegetables too.

Virus

Affects all types of leafy vegetables but most serious on celery and brassicas.

Recognition The overall loss in vigour due to virus attack may be immediately apparent but the tell-tale leaf symptoms of yellowing, puckering and, most characteristic of all, mosaic or mottle-like patterns of paler colour are readily seen. On brassicas, dark brown-black spots may occur.

Possible confusion with aphid attack which may also cause leaf puckering, but when the infestation is severe enough to do this, the insects themselves will be readily apparent. The black spotting on brassicas is impossible to differentiate from leaf spots caused by fungus. The more regular mosaics and mottles are similar to some effects of nutrient deficiency, especially of magnesium or manganese, but such deficiencies tend to affect all plants in a plot, whereas a virus infection is likely to occur on scattered individuals.

Cultural treatment It is important to remove crop debris promptly. This is particularly so with old plants that may remain standing over winter; not only is this an unsound practice generally, but it gives an opportunity for the virus to persist.

Chemical treatment Although viruses cannot be controlled directly by chemicals, it is often possible to limit their impact by controlling the aphids which provide the means of dispersing and introducing them to healthy plants. Thus, the routine use of any of the modern aphid sprays is essential.

General Although some loss of produce may occur because of stunted or yellowed foliage, vegetables infected with virus are perfectly safe to eat – plant viruses don't infect people.

Leaf miners

Affect brassicas, celery and beetroot, though almost every type of garden plant suffers from the attack of species of insect larvae that tunnel between the leaf tissues.

Recognition The leaves display irregular, usually pale markings that betray the tunnelling activities of the pests. Sometimes, especially if a leaf is held up to the light, the larva itself will be seen as a darker mass at the end of one of the tunnels.

Cultural treatment Provided a close watch is maintained on growing crops throughout the season, it may be possible to keep leaf miners in check simply by removing affected leaves as soon as they are seen and destroying them.

Chemical treatment Because the pest is inside the leaf tissues, contact insecticides, even modern ones like permethrin, are of limited use in controlling leaf miners. A systemic chemical such as dimethoate that penetrates into the leaf tissues is much more effective, although it must be remembered that a longer interval must elapse between treatment and harvest.

Whitefly

Affects brassicas.

Recognition The small, white, moth-like brassica whiteflies appear identical to those that infest plants indoors (page 13) and, again, the secondary effects of sticky honeydew and black, sooty, mould growth are often more significant in spoiling the produce.

Cultural treatment As the brassica whitefly, unlike the greenhouse whitefly, can survive outdoors during the winter, it is essential that old vegetable debris is cleared away.

Chemical treatment With all types of whitefly infestation, control is difficult because the juvenile stages of the insects' development are not nearly as susceptible to chemical sprays as are the adults. Regular treatments are called for, therefore, and these should be either with contact insecticides, such as permethrin, or a systemic compound, such as dimethoate.

14. Root Vegetables

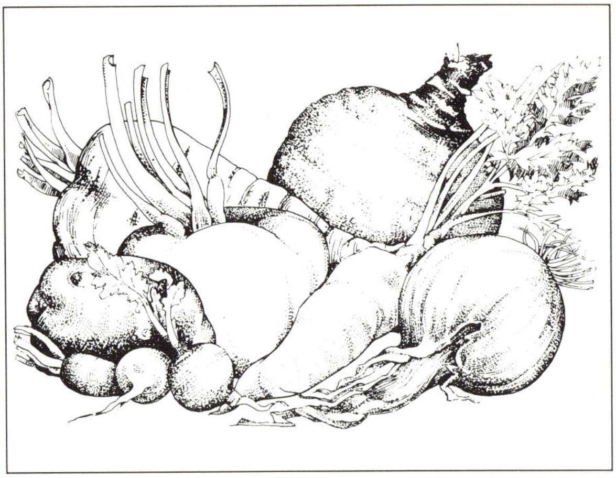

With root vegetables damage occurs where you cannot see it. It is most important to be able to recognise from above-ground parts what is taking place under the soil. Wilting, an odd change of leaf colour, a general stunting or a dark stain spreading up the stem should all arouse suspicion; but confirmation will almost always mean uprooting plants. In this section I consider damage to the roots themselves, but many of the problems of leafy vegetables affect root crops also. The term 'root' has here been extended to include potato tubers and onion bulbs.

Clubroot

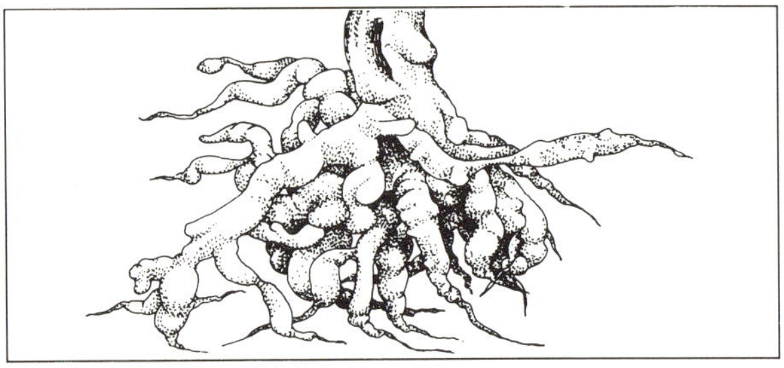

Affects turnips and swedes; also cabbages, cauliflowers, Brussels sprouts, wallflowers, stocks and all other plants of the family Cruciferae.
Recognition The above-ground parts may wilt and appear stunted and the leaves take on the red-purple tint often associated with root damage. In severe attacks, the plants may die but poor growth is the commoner effect. The roots bear irregularly swollen and distorted outgrowths (galls) which ultimately decay.
Possible confusion with cabbage root fly (below) which has similar above-ground symptoms; turnip gall weevil causes galls which contain a small grub; hybridisation nodules look similar but are hard, harmless galls on some varieties of swede and turnip.
Cultural treatment Maintain a long rotation between brassica crops, although this, on its own, will not mean that the disease won't appear. Do not grow brassicas on water-logged soil and ensure that the pH does not fall below 7. Be especially careful not to introduce clubroot into uncontaminated gardens for it is almost impossible to eradicate from the soil; take care, therefore, when borrowing tools and ensure that they are well scrubbed with hot soapy water before use.
Chemical treatment Protect brassica transplants (especially bought plants which may have been in contact with the disease) by treating them with a proprietary root-dip based on calomel or thiophanate-methyl.
Resistant varieties None are wholly reliable but the swedes Chignecto and Wilhelmsburger and the turnips Milan White and Milan Purple Top may be less affected.
General Affected roots must be destroyed, preferably by burning. Tops of leafy brassicas will be quite safe to eat.

Cabbage root fly

Affects turnips and swedes; also cabbages, cauliflowers, Brussels sprouts, wallflowers, stocks and most other plants of the family Cruciferae.
Recognition The plants appear stunted, often with a characteristic red-purple colouration to the leaves. The roots are eaten and tunnelled by white maggots and, if attacked in the early stages, may become dry and shrivelled. In later attacks the surfaces of turnips and swedes become disfigured and irregularly channelled.
Possible confusion with clubroot which results in similar above-ground effects but also causes severe galling of the roots; a shortage of nitrogen fertiliser may also result in reddish, stunted plants, but there are no maggots or root damage.
Cultural treatment Plants planted or sown in spring, especially in May, are at the greatest risk, but a small felt collar placed around each transplant is an effective deterrent to the female flies which lay their eggs on the soil close to the stem base. Such collars are available at garden shops and some are impregnated with insecticide.
Chemical treatment This is never wholly reliable but granular insecticides containing diazinon or

bromophos may be worked into the soil immediately after transplants are put out. If attacks are detected sufficiently early it may be possible to save plants by watering them with a spray strength solution of pirimiphos-methyl.
Resistant varieties None.
General Turnip, swede and radish roots tunnelled by the maggots should be discarded and not eaten.

Flea beetles

Affect turnips, radishes and swedes; occasionally seedlings of other cruciferous plants; related species of flea beetle attack other garden plants.
Recognition Tiny holes appear in the cotyledons and leaves of young plants; sometimes they appear almost sieve-like. Attacks are worst in dry weather in spring and plants may be checked or killed. Sometimes the adult beetles may be seen jumping on and around affected plants.
Cultural treatment Ensure that all crop debris is cleared away promptly to remove sites where the beetles can persist. Ensure also that brassica beds have been well fertilised in advance of sowing or planting and that seedlings are given adequate water.
Chemical treatment Sprinkle derris or HCH dust on and around emerging seedlings.

Carrot fly

Affects carrots and, to a lesser extent, parsnips, parsley and celery.
Recognition Above-ground parts of plants may be stunted and the leaves are characteristically reddened. The roots are tunnelled by small, whitish maggots.
Possible confusion with other forms of root damage and some types of virus; these may cause the foliage to turn red, but no maggots are present.
Cultural treatment Carrot fly control is exceedingly difficult. By delaying sowing until early June, it may be possible to avoid the period when most of the females are egg laying. Disturbance of carrot foliage releases an aroma that attracts the flies and sowing sparingly to minimise the amount of thinning needed will help limit this. Watering immediately after any thinning will help to remove the aromatic chemicals also. Do not leave carrots in the ground longer than necessary and don't attempt to store them in the ground if fly attacks have been experienced during the season.
Chemical treatment This is never very effective, but soil application of bromophos or diazinon granules before sowing may give some protection.
Resistant varieties None.
General It is often possible to tolerate a small amount of damage if an extra row of plants is grown to compensate for the wastage.

Onion white rot

Affects onions, garlic, leeks, shallots, chives and related ornamental *Allium* species. Almost always the most severe attacks arise on spring onions.
Recognition Small groups of plants display yellow leaves and stunted growth. Sometimes the plants fall over because the decayed roots give them inadequate support. A matted, cotton-wool like growth envelops the bulb.
Possible confusion with botrytis or onion fly, which may cause leaves to turn yellow, but no cottony mould forms. Mould on onion bulbs in store is caused by neck rot (page 53), which requires quite different treatment.
Cultural treatment Maintain a three or four-year rotation of onion crops if possible; remove promptly any diseased plants found, together with several spadesful of the surrounding soil, especially if the disease has not appeared on the land previously. Such contaminated material is best disposed of by burial in a deep hole.
Chemical treatment Add fungicidal dust containing benomyl, thiophanate-methyl or calomel to the drill before sowing as a preventive treatment; but do not expect 100% control if the soil is at all badly contaminated. Steep garlic cloves and shallot or onion sets for 30 minutes in spray-strength benomyl or thiophanate-methyl before planting – this is especially important on clean land as white rot is very easily introduced on such plants.

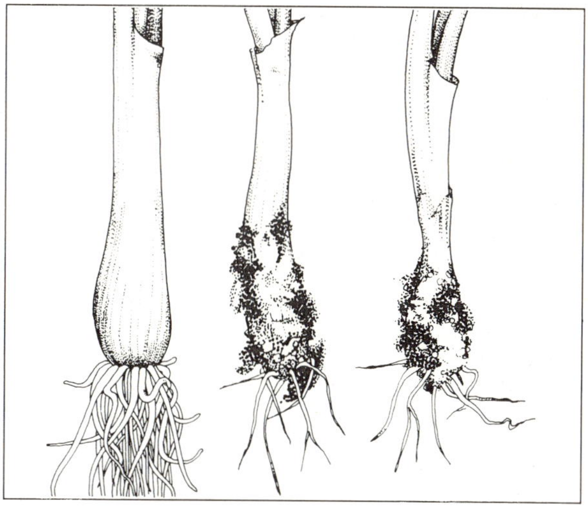

A healthy and two diseased onions

Resistant varieties None.
General None of the treatments for white rot is entirely satisfactory and if the soil becomes really severely affected, then raising spring onions in large pots may be the only solution.

Potato blight

Affects potatoes and outdoor tomatoes.
Recognition The foliage bears very dark brown or black blotches, usually with a thin white mould on the undersides. In damp weather, these effects spread very rapidly until the bulk of the foliage and stems becomes a softened, black mass. The potato tubers bear brown surface lesions with a characteristic red-brown speckling within. They are inedible.
Possible confusion with grey mould. This may sometimes affect potato foliage, especially if it has been bruised by, for example, gardeners walking between the rows. It is, however, much more limited in extent than blight. Other types of rot also affect the tubers but the red-brown colour of blight is characteristic.
Cultural treatment Never dump old potato tubers in gardens – if they are infected, the sprouts will be diseased and blight will spread to the new crop. Thus, when old haulm is composted, cut off any tubers and bury them separately.
Chemical treatment In damp summers, it is wise to apply a fortnightly protective spray of mancozeb to potato crops (or of dust to tomatoes), starting at the beginning of July, but in hot, dry seasons, infection is most unlikely to occur and the treatment is unnecessary. Wash treated tomatoes before eating.
Resistant varieties None; some, including the popular King Edward, are especially susceptible.

Common scab

Affects potatoes, beetroot, swedes, turnips and radish.
Recognition Roots or tubers are more or less covered by rough, scab-like lesions with somewhat irregular edges, although the actual vigour and yield of the plants are little affected. Scab occurs most severely on light, free-draining, alkaline soils; similar symptoms on potatoes on wet, heavy soils are the result of attack by powdery scab, a quite different disease.
Possible confusion with skin spot and wart disease. Mild attacks of common scab may be confused with a relatively harmless problem known as skin spot, whereas severe attacks of powdery scab in which outgrowths develop on potatoes in store might be mistaken for the very serious, but now uncommon, wart disease.
Treatment There is no chemical control for either form of scab and, when attacks are light, the only significant result is the inconvenience of the extra peeling necessary. Nonetheless, certain precautions may sensibly be taken to minimise damage by common scab; never dispose of scabby tubers on the compost heap, never lime soil on which crops have been attacked, and dig in quantities of lawn mowings or other green matter. If severe attacks have been experienced in the previous season, it would be wise to water the crop as the tubers are swelling to prevent the soil drying out. Some potato varieties are definitely less prone than others to common scab and might profitably be grown where the disease has been troublesome; among these are King Edward, Pentland Crown and Arran Pilot.
Powdery scab is generally less common and more difficult to control. Improving the drainage and a long rotation are the only practicable measures.

Misshapen roots

Badly formed roots, with no apparent pest or disease cause, constitute probably the most frequent problem on carrots and parsnips. The malformation may adopt several guises but commonest of all is the development of bifurcations or forks, generally known as fanging. There are normally three possible causes, all of which are features of the soil conditions and all of which are fairly readily put right. The cause most often cited is that fresh farmyard manure has been applied too close to sowing time; the general guideline here is that it should not be applied more closely than in advance of the preceding crop. The second most frequent cause is simply that the crop is being grown on unsuitable or inadequately prepared land; the soil must be free-draining and of a fine tilth with no large clods or stones to impede root growth. The third cause is often the most puzzling for it applies to soils with no fresh manure and which are light and free-draining. Here, however, root development is affected by the formation of a 'pan' or hard layer several inches beneath the soil surface, as a result of the deposition of minerals washed down by prolonged rainfall. Deep and thorough cultivation will break up this layer.

Sometimes carrot roots are prone to vertical splitting. Like the splitting of tomatoes, cabbage heads, apples and other produce, this usually results from renewed growth following a dry period. It can be avoided by ensuring that the plants are watered regularly.

Virus

Affects all forms of root vegetables, but the most important are the viruses infecting potatoes.
Recognition Most commonly, the effects of viruses are the insidious ones of a gradual decline, year by year, in crop vigour and yield if seed tubers are saved for replanting. Sometimes, but not always, more obvious visual symptoms accompany this decline; for example, upward rolling of the leaves (the lower leaves first), which often have a brittle texture; dark streaks along the leaf veins; or mottling or other pale

green or yellowish patterns on the leaves.
Possible confusion with little else – the leaf symptoms are quite unique and characteristic, but before ascribing a poor crop to virus infection, check that overall soil fertility isn't to blame and remember that virus is most unlikely to affect severely plants raised from fresh, certified seed.

Treatment To be certain of avoiding virus problems, the golden rule is always to buy new, certified seed tubers each season. These will have been grown in northern regions where virus-carrying aphids are sparse, although good aphid control in the garden is still important as the plants develop.

Soft rot (and black leg)

Affects all root vegetables, but it is probably most common on swedes. Black leg is a disease of potatoes with many features in common with soft rot.
Recognition The plant appears stunted and debilitated and, when pulled up, the bulbous roots or tubers are found to have more or less disintegrated into a foul-smelling, semi-liquid state; quite commonly, the outer skin remains as a shell with the contents all but disappeared. The symptoms of black leg on potatoes are an inward rolling of the upper leaves and a black, slimy appearance to the stem base.
Possible confusion with few other rotting diseases in the garden, although stored potatoes may be subject to a number of similar problems (page 52).
Treatment In common with most diseases caused by bacteria, there is no chemical treatment available for these conditions. Both can be minimised by not planting potatoes or other root crops on land liable to water-logging and by ensuring that seed tubers are sound and healthy. Too heavy an application of manure or nitrogen fertiliser can predispose plants to soft rotting. The variety King Edward tends to be less prone to attack by black leg than many varieties. Notes on the avoidance of soft rot and other decay problems in stored produce are given on page 52.

Eelworms

Affect many types of plant, but among root vegetables, the attacks of cyst eelworm on potatoes constitute the only serious problems.
Recognition Plants generally show poor growth and yellowed foliage and, in a large plot of potatoes, the attack may be revealed as a discrete group of discoloured and stunted plants among healthy ones. The diagnostic symptom is only seen when the plants are dug, however – groups of minute white or yellowish marble-like bodies on the roots.
Cultural treatment Routine rotation of potato crops will help keep the likelihood of eelworm attacks to a minimum although, once damage has occured, it may be necessary to avoid growing potatoes (or tomatoes, which can be attacked also) for at least six years to allow the infestation to die down.
Chemical treatment None.
Resistant varieties Pentland Javelin and Maris Piper are probably the best early and maincrop potatoes respectively if land is infested with the species of eelworm that produces the tiny yellow bodies. Unfortunately, they are not resistant to the species that produces the tiny white bodies.

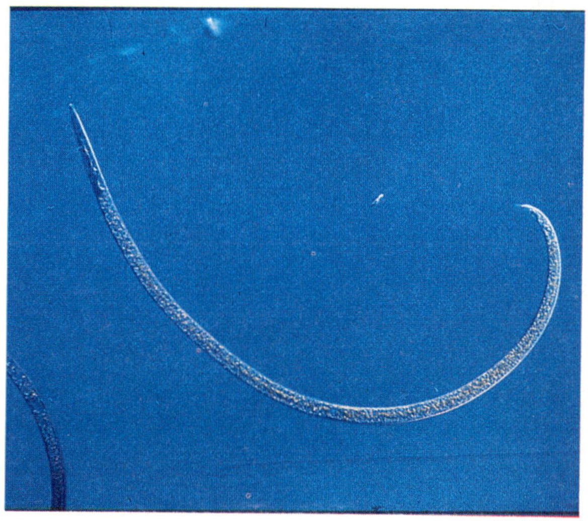

Eelworm magnified × 80 approx.

Parsnip canker

Affects parsnips.
Recognition There are several different causes of parsnip canker and they result in a range of effects, from a purple-black decay that spreads from the small lateral roots, to large purple lesions with a soft colourless margin, and rough orange-brown patches around the shoulder of the root.
Possible confusion with other root-rotting problems, especially soft rot where the entire root becomes soft and squashy, and violet root rot, where the root becomes enmeshed with dark stringy growths.
Cultural treatment Try to maintain a four-year rotation between parsnip crops. Earth up parsnips in summer to prevent the fungus from reaching the roots, and try sowing later (early May) to produce smaller roots, which are less prone to attack. Always avoid growing parsnips on water-logged ground.
Chemical treatment None.
Resistant varieties Avonresister is unaffected by any of the forms of parsnip canker and should be chosen if the disease has appeared in a previous season.

15. Problems in Greenhouses

The greenhouse is a very different environment from the rest of the garden in the protection, warmth and general cossetting that it provides for our plants. Unfortunately, it provides these benefits for pests and diseases too; all-year round plants mean all-year round aphids and mildew also. Similarly, in keeping exotic and tender plants, we are also providing conditions for exotic and tender pests that wouldn't stand a chance outside in the garden. All these are very good reasons for paying particular attention and care to general hygiene in the greenhouse and making up for the natural, seasonal control that the winter would normally provide.

Among the pests and diseases that occur in greenhouses but are very troublesome outdoors too are botrytis grey mould, damping off, mildew, soft rot, sooty moulds, virus, aphids, caterpillars, earwigs, thrips and woodlice. Advice on these will be found in earlier sections of the book. House plant problems (see page 12) occurring commonly in the greenhouse are fungus gnats, mealy bugs and scale insects, while leaf mould, red spider mites and whitefly are almost always more serious in greenhouses than elsewhere. On these pages, some general guidance is given therefore on greenhouse management and design in relation to maintaining healthy plants.

Greenhouse design and construction

An enormous range of styles of greenhouse is now available but probably the major factor from a pest and disease standpoint is the effectiveness of the ventilation. Damp, stagnant air, especially at floor level, is an invitation to rot and decay so, when buying a new greenhouse, pay particular attention to the presence of vents low down, as well as in the roof.

It is sometimes said that wooden greenhouses are more difficult to clean and disinfect and that they contain more nooks and crannies to harbour pests. This isn't really true however; it is the thoroughness with which the structure is cleaned that matters and, indeed, aluminium greenhouses have the disadvantage that the metal framework can be damaged if sulphur fumigant candles are used in them.

Management

Cleanliness is the prerequisite for healthiness in the greenhouse and a sound routine of annual disinfection is essential. This must be done when the greenhouse is empty of plants and the most convenient time is probably in the autumn when large, immovable crops such as tomatoes and cucumbers are finished for the season, but when the weather is still warm so that the perennial occupants won't suffer from being placed outside for a day or so. If all the plants are in pots, however, the operation is best done in late summer. The entire fabric of the house and staging should be washed thoroughly with soap, water and a proprietary disinfectant.

Cleanliness means more than this major annual shake-down however, and the importance of watching for the first signs of pest or disease and applying the appropriate treatment promptly cannot be overstressed. Make use of 'smoke' or fumigant formulations of fungicides and insecticides when these are available but remember that the vents and door must be closed and the entire structure be leak-proof for the technique to work effectively. It is equally important to be scrupulous in the removal of dead leaves and flower heads; this is not simply a matter of tidiness, for such dead tissues are breeding grounds for problems, in particular for the grey mould fungus, botrytis, which will rapidly spread from them to healthy plants.

Water is an ever-important commodity in the greenhouse and many gardeners have a rain-water butt to collect water from the roof. Be cautious when using this water in the greenhouse, however, for the warm conditions may incubate any pest or disease organisms that it contains and cause them to multiply to damaging levels. It is important that if rain-water is to be used in this way, the butt should be covered with a close-fitting lid.

Not only do greenhouse plants need water; they need feeding too, but here also, a word of caution. Be very wary indeed about using farm-yard manure on tomato or cucumber plants, for the straw that it contains may well have derived from cereal crops that have been sprayed with weed-killer. This weed-killer, even in minute amounts, can persist and cause the plants to become distorted and worthless.

A cautionary note too concerning the use of the border soil in a greenhouse. Whilst many gardeners now grow greenhouse crops in containers of various sorts (including, of course, growing bags), some still use the original soil. Although this is usually a safe practice with crops such as lettuce, it is tempting fate with tomatoes as the fungi that cause wilt can easily build up with repeated cropping and, once present, are almost impossible to eradicate. A switch to container production or, possibly to using grafted tomatoes with a wilt-resistant rootstock is then the only solution.

One apparently curious matter of personal hygiene should not go unmentioned; smokers should desist from indulging in the habit in the greenhouse for cigarette tobacco may contain a tobacco virus that, although harmless to humans, can be spread, by fingers, to tomato plants and cause a devastating disease.

Finally, a note about biological control of greenhouse pests. Gardeners will often see reference to this technique, in which a parasitic or predatory species is introduced into the greenhouse to control a pest species. Although successful in commercial practice, the resuls are nonetheless usually disappointing or short-lived on a small scale.

A. Tight fitting roof ventilators, capable of being opened at least to 45 degrees. These act with the base ventilators to permit through-flow of air and prevent diseases from developing in stagnant conditions. The tight fitting is essential to prevent leaking of fumigant vapours.

B. Basal ventilators. These are often overlooked but they are necessary to prevent the build-up of stagnant air at floor level, which will lead to stem and leaf rotting problems.

C. Butt for rain water. This must have a tight fitting lid to prevent algal and other growth from building up within. Because of the warmth within the greenhouse, which will incubate any pest or disease organisms, it is sensible only to use water from rain butts outdoors and to use tap water within the greenhouse itself.

D. Pots and plant containers must always be scrubbed and disinfected after use. This is especially so if they are to be stored in the greenhouse where any pests or diseases that they harbour may be spread to growing plants.

E. Tight fitting door to prevent escape of fumigant vapours and keep out mice or other pests.

F. Growing bag for tomatoes or other crops. This is a more reliable way of raising such plants than in the border soil of the greenhouse where wilt and rot-causing fungi will almost certainly build up after a few crops.

G. Slatted benches for ease of cleaning. Once a year, the entire house should be cleared and disinfected thoroughly.

H Pot plants on the bench. Almost inevitably, the greenhouse will be used for raising a wide variety of different types of plant, some requiring more shade and less humidity than others. Do ensure that plants are placed within the greenhouse in the most beneficial position.

I. The glass panes of the greenhouse must be kept clean; not only will they harbour potential disease organisms but, in obstructing the light, they may place plants under stress. Conversely, in summer, shading should be used on the sunny side to prevent similar stress.

16. Storage Problems with Fruit and Vegetables

Few things in gardening are more disheartening than to see a bumper crop safely collected and put into store, only to be lost through rot, decay or pest activity in the ensuing weeks. In this account, with one notable exception, the principal problems likely to be encountered in stored produce are not described in detail and it must be admitted that, in most cases, finding actual damage means that it is then too late to do very much about it. General guidelines are given, therefore, on the handling of produce intended for store and also on the conditions under which storage should be made. Further detail on the control of some of the pest and disease problems that will compound the storage problems if allowed to go unchecked while the plants are still growing are described in the appropriate fruit and vegetable sections elsewhere in the book. The one exception, neck rot of onions, is a special case and is considered on the next page.

Although concerned primarily with edible produce, much of what is said here is equally applicable to stored bulbs, corms and tubers of ornamentals.

Careful handling means less damage

In commercial practice, a dramatic increase has been noted in recent years of losses through decay of fruit and vegetables where modern developments have permitted the gradual phasing out of labour-intensive harvesting and sorting by hand in favour of mechanical harvesting and grading machines. There is a lesson to be learned here for the gardener for, although undoubtedly quicker than mere men, these extraordinarily ingenious devices do not possess the gentle touch that the slow old human hand affords. Thus they bump and they bruise; they remove small pieces of skin or peel and they knock off immature buds. And nothing so predisposes fruit and vegetables to decay as damage such as this; these wounds provide the entry points for fungi and bacteria to infect and the starting places for pests to nibble. Thus, if there is one golden rule, it must be that any garden produce intended for long or even short term storage must be collected and handled with the greatest care.

Do's and Don'ts

- Don't store windfall apples or pears.
- Don't drop any fruit that is to be stored, either onto the ground or even into the collecting basket.
- Don't pull the stalk from fruit that is to be stored; this will cause quite sufficient wounding for infection to occur.
- If vegetables have to be washed before storage, do this with the greatest care; ensure that they are well dried afterwards, but don't do this by exposing them to any form of heat – including the sun.
- Don't attempt to store any produce that already shows the merest sign of pest or disease attack.
- Grade for size; smaller fruit and vegetables commonly keep better and longer than larger ones.
- Ensure that bulbs or corms lifted from the ground for storage are well dried by arranging them on slatted trays in a well-ventilated shed or outhouse. Carefully rub away any dry soil and dead leaves and then reject any showing disease or pest blemishes.
- Always harvest produce when it is at, or just below the peak of maturity.
- Remember that some vegetables (carrots, beetroot and swedes for instance) may well be better left where they are, to store in the ground with straw or other covering as frost protection.
- If vegetables have to be trimmed or cut (to remove leaves, for instance) always do this with a clean knife.
- If you intend to grow crops specifically for storing, always choose varieties listed in catalogues as suitable for this purpose – some, for example, have very much thicker skins than others.

Storage in the correct conditions is more than half the battle against rot

Even if crops have been harvested and selected carefully, losses can still occur simply through neglecting the way in which they are placed in the store and, indeed, the nature of the storage place itself.

The storage building should preferably be one that is not subject to frequent disturbance that will lead to wide fluctuations in temperature and humidity; a garden shed is normally suitable but garages or other buildings where toxic fumes might taint the produce are much less so. If possible, install extra ventilators close to ground level and do not stack bags or trays of fruit and vegetables against the cold, north wall.

Try to ensure that the building is rodent proof; in some years, wood mice and voles reach almost plague proportions and invade fruit and vegetable stores, gaining access through the smallest holes.

There are, of course, optimum conditions for each and every type of produce, but below you will see how crops harvested from a vegetable and fruit garden might be stored in a small shed.

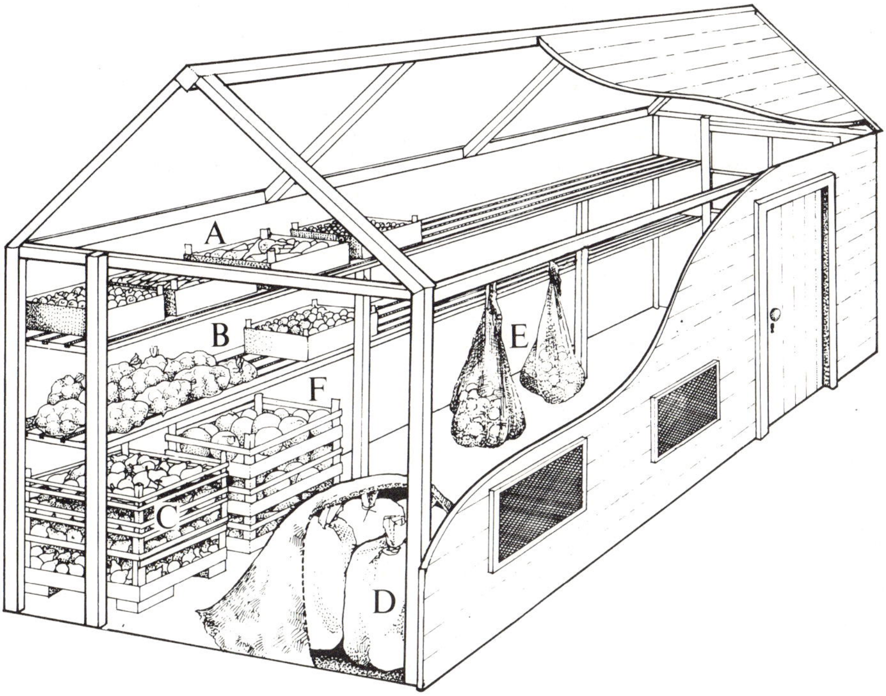

A. – Store each type of fruit or vegetable separately.
B. – Store apples – a dozen at a time – in plastic bags with tiny holes for ventilation.
C. – Store pears individually on slatted trays.
D. – Store potatoes in paper sacks, preferably of double thickness, and covered with insulation against frost.
E. – Store onions or ornamental bulbs on slatted trays (up to two layers deep) or hung in nets.
F. – Root vegetables not stored in the ground should be placed in layers in well ventilated wooden boxes with sand between each layer.

Neck rot

Affects onions, shallots.
Recognition The neck of the bulb softens and a grey-green mould growth gradually spreads down to affect the entire bulb which becomes brown and worthless.
Possible confusion with superficially similar decay that may occur on all manner of other types of vegetables and fruit in store but it should be appreciated that onion neck rot is very different from all other conditions in that, although it cannot be cured, its occurrence may be prevented by the most improbable of techniques.
Treatment The fungus responsible for onion neck rot has its origin on the onion seed and it grows quite invisibly on the onion while it is maturing in the garden. The treatment to prevent the problem therefore is to dust the seed with either benomyl or thiophante-methyl before sowing. Sets should be soaked in spray strength chemical for about 30 minutes as described for ornamental bulbs on page 19. As an added precaution, old onions should not be dumped in the garden but disposed of elsewhere.

17. First Aid

This and the following three pages are an attempt to provide a 'First Aid' manual for the ailing plant and its owner. They differ from the Key at the front of the book in that they do not, in most instances, help you directly to identify a problem, nor necessarily to understand how the problem is caused or how its recurrence may be prevented; although the suggested action may sometimes be of self-evident value in this regard. Thus, there is little reference to protective treatments, to garden hygiene or to pest and disease prevention. My concern here is with the sudden happening or the sudden discovery (perhaps after returning from holiday), that something has gone seriously wrong. I have adopted therefore, an analogy to the 'scene of accident' procedure, where there is little merit in telling somone lying on the kerbside that the way to avoid being knocked down is to look both ways before crossing the road! What is needed is quickly to determine the nature of the damage and to treat the symptom rather than the cause with first aid and even a little sympathy.

Fortunately, an ailing plant, compared with an animal or person, usually has time on its side. It is unlikely to succumb within half an hour, whatever its condition (although even here, there are one or two exceptions), but in every case of misfortune, the faster a remedy can be applied, the better. And although every possible accident or misfortune cannot be catered for, I have selected, in no particular order, those that seem to occur most frequently.

Is it dead?

It is surprising how many people simply fail to believe the evidence of death before them. Nonetheless, it does not pay to be too glib for appearances can sometimes be deceptive. Brown and shrivelled leaves will themselves be dead and will not revive but the stem that bears them may well be living and healthy. Indeed, the leaf fall itself may be a quite natural event; do make sure that the plant causing you all the worry isn't a deciduous species undergoing normal autumnal leaf fall, or even a herbaceous perennial in the process of dying down to a rootstock for the winter. If in doubt with woody plants (and this is especially likely to be so if the plant has failed to produce any leaves in the spring when its colleagues are turning attractively green), scrape away a little of the bark with a finger nail. If the underlying tissues are green, all is well; if they are dark brown or black, all is dead and if they are somewhere in between, something is wrong somewhere but the best plan it to leave well alone and let nature take its course, one way or the other.

Someone has trodden on it.

It happens all the time; the careless step backwards while digging the border, the small child allowed rather too much free rein, or even the great dane with a single exuberant bound. All stand a fair chance of landing on a plant, of snapping a stem and causing consternation all round; the consternation being in direct proportion to the size, the age and cost of the plant. If the plant is woody and the stem isn't totally severed, a repair job may be effected by binding the wound very tightly with electrician's tape. If the stem is fleshy, this is a pointless exercise for the stem will only shrivel and perhaps allow rot to set in. Nonetheless the loss of stem either woody or fleshy is unlikely to result in the total demise of any perennial plant which should be carefully cut back to the next bud. A large proportion of the growth may have been lost, but provided the rootstock hasn't been squashed flat, the plant should survive. Annual plants with no rootstock from which to shoot are a different matter however and, once trodden on, they are best discarded.

There are holes in the leaves.

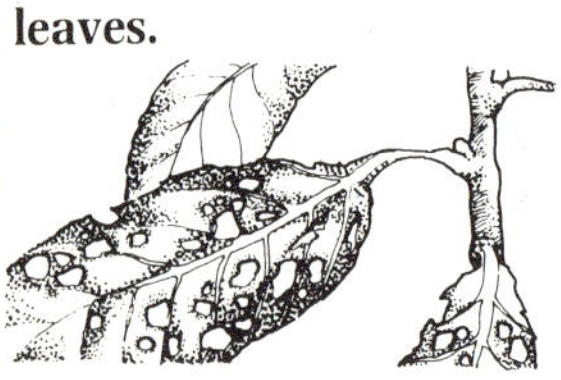

Holes of varying kinds, shapes and sizes can appear in leaves very suddenly. You are quite sure that they weren't there at the last time you looked; and you are very probably right. In almost all cases, some insect larva will be responsible and has probably hatched out from eggs that were lying invisibly on the leaves the last time that you saw the plant. There is no real need to know which insect is responsible; spray with the modern contact insecticide permethrin and the problem should be solved, on vegetables, fruit or ornamentals.

There are spots on the leaves.

Whereas holes in leaves are almost always due to insect attack, spots are most likely to be the result of infection by a leaf-spotting fungus. In many cases, the response is to do nothing for the effect may be nothing more than cosmetic and the unnecessary use of chemical sprays is to be discouraged. In a few instances, if left unchecked, more serious damage may ensue, but nothing will happen very quickly. Use the Key and the illustrations therefore to track down the specific problem and take appropriate action.

The rain (or wind) has flattened them.

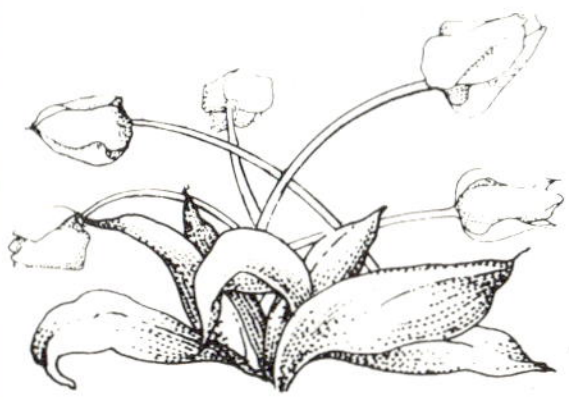

'Them' in this context usually means flowering perennials, for so many of our modern garden flowers have been bred with relatively enormous blooms and stems barely capable of supporting them – tulips, dahlias and paeonies spring to mind. Whilst dahlias and paeonies should be staked routinely, this is not normally considered necessary with tulips but when heavy rain strikes, especially combined with strong wind, the consequence is the almost inevitable flattening. In many instances, the remedy is to do nothing until the plants have restored themselves naturally to a reasonably upright position. If any have been broken, they should be removed but the remainder are best not forced into an upright stance. Once they are reasonably vertical however, canes should be used for support, taking care not to spear the bulb or rootstock as they are inserted, and soft string used for tying.

The flowers (or fruit) have dropped off.

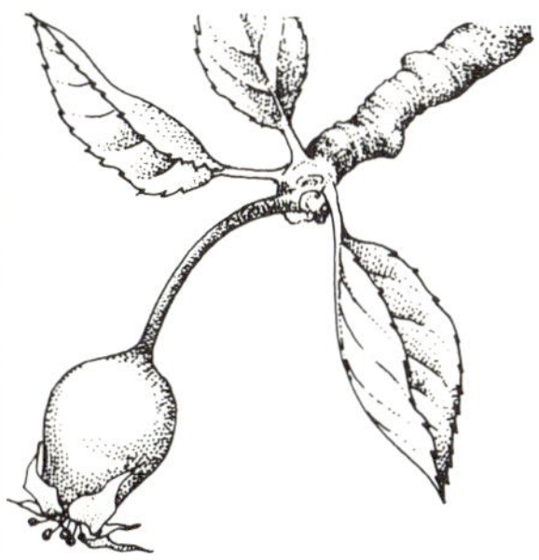

Whereas the shortage of water discussed on page 56 will cause flowers, as well as leaves to droop and, indeed, may result in fruit drop, the response of blossom and fruits to water shortage can be much less obvious. A short-fall in available water that is not serious enough to result in leaves wilting can be quite sufficient to induce fruit to separate from a tree or shrub. There is no immediate remedy (nothing will put them back again!) but the indication is that the plant should be very well mulched in readiness for the next season. Occasionally, pest or disease attack can result in fruit dropping prematurely and, on many apple varieties, concern is often caused as a result of the 'June drop' when, around the middle of June, the tree sheds itself of the excess fruitlets that it doesn't have the capacity to mature. Strong winds, of course, will also bring about premature fruit fall and, in an exposed garden, the erection or planting of some permanent type of wind-break is sensible.

It has gone mouldy.

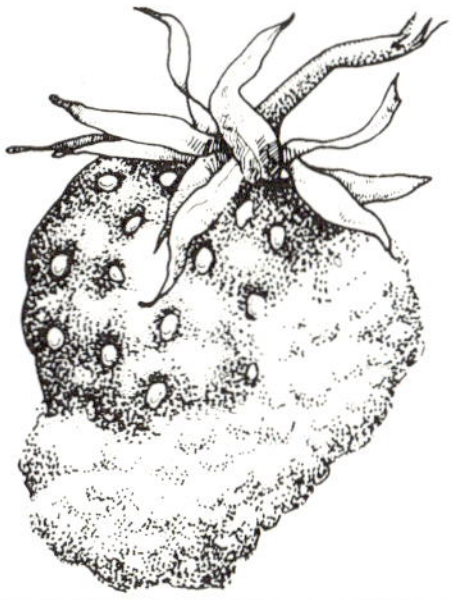

Mouldy is one of those terms that has a very specific meaning in horticulture but which is used colloquially by gardeners to mean any form of fungal growth on plants or plant produce. If such growth is found on plants growing in the garden, the chances are that it is due either to a mildew attack or to botrytis grey mould. Both are most readily controlled by a spray with one of the systemic fungicides, benomyl or thiophanate-methyl, and although it is unwise to use any chemical as a first resort, this is one of those instances where it is justifiable; once infection has reached the stage of appreciable mould growth being present, quick action is called for. If these treatments fail to have any effect, refer to the Key. On fruits and vegetables in store, chemicals should, however, quite definitely not be used; throw the affected produce away and check others nearby for any signs of damage. Details regarding healthy storage are given on page 52.

There are cobwebs on the plants.

Most people imagine that the presence of cobwebs indicates the presence of spiders. On plants however, the cause is most likely to be an attack by another eight-legged creature, the red spider mite. Once the attack has reached a 'festooning' stage, nothing can be done and the plant should be disposed of rapidly. A mild attack may be checked by a fine misting with water. See page 34.

A branch has broken off.

Winter gales are the commonest cause of the snapping of branches from trees, although furniture vans passing down narrow driveways are probably the next most frequent. Whatever the cause, however, the result will be a jagged stump where once the branch grew. This stump must be removed cleanly; not flush with the stem as is often suggested, but flush with the 'collar', the small raised portion at the base. Actually cutting into this collar will remove the wound healing tissues of the plant. Use a fine toothed saw and then treat the wound with a wound sealing compound containing the fungicide thiophanate-methyl.

If the affected branch is seen to be rotten, with decay extending into the trunk, a competent tree surgeon should be consulted to determine the likelihood of the remainder blowing down, with consequently greater problems.

The leaves are drooping (slightly).

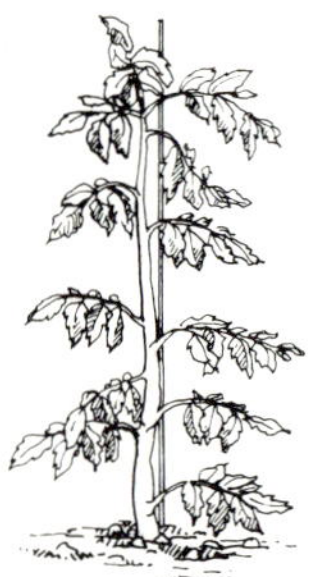

Going away for the weekend in the height of summer can be a dangerous escape, especially when, on Saturday night, someone remembers to ask who last watered the tomatoes; and when. As it becomes apparent they were last attended to sometime around Tuesday morning, the sequence of events becomes predictable and culminates in the plants being found on Sunday evening to be looking decidedly poorly. Of course, it doesn't need to be the tomatoes, but few other plants seem quite so vulnerable, especially if they are in growing bags or pots, and entirely dependent on us for their water supply. Usually, a few days of neglect can be put right by immediately supplying gallons of water and, if this has to be done in the heat of the day, by removing the plants to a shady spot if they are small enough to permit this, or by applying some form of shading to them. You may well find that flowering and fruiting will be set back a week or so and, with tomatoes, that some fruit will be lost to blossom end rot (see page 41) but at least the plants should recover.

The leaves are drooping (severely).

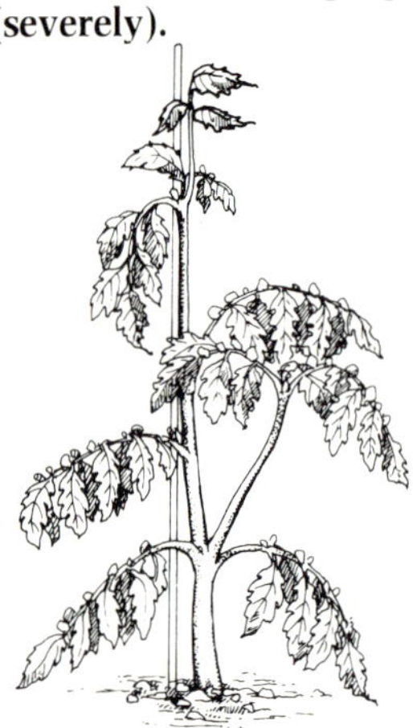

If a plant has been left too long without water, irreparable damage will be caused to its tissues and the time for this to happen varies with different plants. Some, such as certain cacti or aspidistras can tolerate a very prolonged drought indeed, whereas others, such as those succulents like balsams with brittle stems can be killed very quickly in hot weather. Obviously, apply water generously but if after a day the leaves show no signs of recovery, the portents are ominous. It may be worth cutting down perennials to the rootstock in the hope that they may shoot again from the base, but don't be over-optimistic. If leaves are found wilting severely when the plant is in wet compost or soil and water shortage is clearly not to blame, the chances are that the plant's roots have become too wet and decay has set in. Remove the plant, if in a pot, to a drier situation (removing the drainage obstruction if one is present) and then, after a few days when the compost has begun to dry out, run a spray strength solution of benomyl fungicide through the pot, repeating every four or five days until success is achieved or the plant expires.

Except in the most abnormal drought, trees and shrubs are unlikely to wilt though water shortage and so if one is found drooping in this way, the drench around the roots with benomyl may be sufficient to control the soil fungi responsible.

The leaves have gone a funny colour.

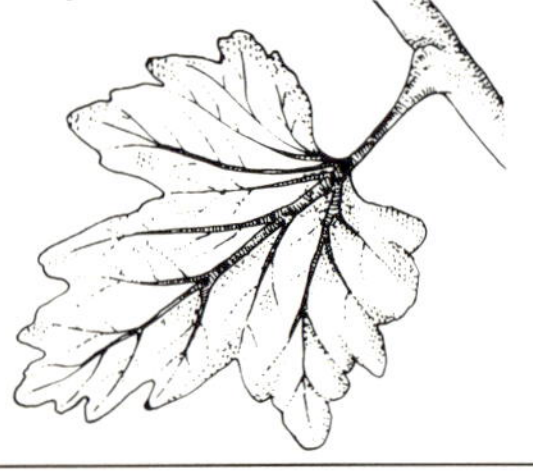

The question to ask here is how funny the colour is, for the causes will be different in different circumstances. If the leaves have turned red, this indicates root stress which may be no more than dryness in the soil, or might indicate pest or disease attack from the soil (use the Key). If a hint of blue or mauve occurs with the red, this is often an indication of a shortage of nitrogen fertiliser (use a liquid feed for a quick response). Yellowing may be the result of overwatering, too little light (is it a house plant too far from a window?) or the first stage of normal seasonal leaf death. Yellowing with the veins remaining green is most often a shortage of iron on chalky soil and the remedy here is to use a liquid formulation of sequestrene.

Rover (or Fido, or little Johnny) has done it on the lawn.	If you have actually seen the culprit in action, then the cause of the brown patch of grass will be self-evident; urine is a fairly powerful grass killer, especially if it originates with lady dogs. The second most common cause of this discrete brown patchiness is carelessly spilt petrol when lawnmowers are being filled. In all cases, the remedy is the same – either wait for new grass to colonise the dead area (which will take a long time) or cut out the affected patch and re-sow or re-turf.

A note on trees

Trees take a long time to grow to maturity and although you may own the land on which your garden trees are growing, you may not necessarily be able to cut them down or chop them up at will. Large and choice specimen trees may be protected by a Tree Preservation Order taken out by your local authority, whose permission will be needed before you can fell or even lop them. Even if your tree isn't specifically protected, you may live in a designated Conservation Area in which all trees above a certain height and girth may not be interfered with before you obtain authority to do so. Only if a tree is dead or in a dangerous condition may you act on your own initiative. Nonetheless, even the unfortunate cedar shown below may not be beyond some form of redemption. Clearly nothing will put the top back, But the remainder may not actually be deemed dangerous. In all such instances, it is wise to check with your local authority before taking out the saw or axe.

One has to be realistic – nothing will put it back.

18. Traditional Remedies

Many gardeners, for perfectly sound practical reasons such as cost, or on more fundamental moral grounds, object to the use of modern chemical measures for pest and disease control. Whilst there is no reason for finding pesticides any more objectionable than other intrusions of synthetic chemicals on our everyday lives, I would not dispute that they should be a second choice if other techniques fail. Some garden problems that are particularly difficult to combat have, over many years, attracted a bevy of home-spun remedies ranging from the evidently logical, if obscure, to the blatantly bizarre. The problems that come especially into this category are clubroot, honey fungus, whitefly, eelworms, moles, slugs, cats, peach leaf curl, apple scab, aphids and mildew. Some of the suggested remedies for these afflictions are given in this section which does not, by any means claim to be exhaustive – much less, reliable!

Clubroot

Books could, and indeed have, been written on the control of clubroot and treatments have ranged from such sensible measures as liming the land to such ludicrous proposals as watering a 1 to 500 mixture of petrol and liquid manure at the rate of $2\frac{1}{2}$ gals per square yard. Consistently, the use of a small stick of rhubarb inserted into the planting hole is claimed to be beneficial, with egg-shells, soot and mothballs as slightly less reliable alternatives. The egg shells presumably work by raising the soil pH and the mothballs might just be effective through the general, toxic properties of naphthalene. Soot has quite commonly been proposed as a pesticide and, as it contains a wide range of by-products of carbon combustion, it is conceivable that some might be fungicidal; although whether they are any more environmentally acceptable than a synthetic, purpose-made pesticide is arguable. Garlic features in clubroot control too, as it does with several other diseases and although some of the chemicals that it is known to contain might have fungicidal properties, it seems rather improbable that they are present in sufficient quantities to make much impression. The rhubarb story, because it is so widespread, is difficult either to counter or to support. Scientific tests have been made but have been inconclusive and, logically, it might be thought that the highly acid nature of rhubarb sap would favour rather than suppress the disease.

Honey fungus

The commonest suggestion in this context is to use creosote, either to cure an already diseased plant or to kill the fungus in the soil and prevent infection from occurring. Neither has proved reliable when tested and as creosote is so damaging to plant life, it should not be experimented with.

Eelworms

Perhaps because they are virtually invisible, eelworms have attracted a fair share of possible remedies. The commonest is one that comes under the general heading of companion planting, which takes as its thesis the notion that certain types of plant grow more satisfactorily or are less likely to become diseased or infected if they are placed close to certain other species. In general, there is little scientific evidence to support the notion (although this does not mean that all the claims are invalid; merely unproven). The protection of plants liable to eelworm attack by planting Tagetes (Marigolds) nearby has some basis however for certain, but not all (and certainly not potato cyst eelworm) forms of eelworm are affected by the root secretions.

Peach leaf curl

Garlic features here for it is claimed that growing garlic under peach trees protects them from leaf curl. It is scarcely conceivable that anything produced by the garlic could permeate the branches in sufficient quantities to have any effect, but it may not be coincidence that the seasons that favour good garlic (hot, dry weather) are precisely those that inhibit peach leaf curl development. Hanging moth balls among the leaves has also been suggested, but it is impossible to become very excited about this either.

Aphids

The simplest control for aphids is to nip off the affected shoots or to hose off the insects with a powerful jet of water. Once again, garlic rears its cloves, for roses can, supposedly, be kept free from infestation by growing garlic nearby. I can vouch for the failure of this approach in at least one garden. Woolly aphid on apple trees is said to be checked by growing one of the trailing varieties of nasturtium through the branches. No doubt a very pretty concept but doubtfully trustworthy.

Whitefly

The nasturtium concept has been ingeniously adapted to greenhouse use – grow nasturtiums in the greenhouse and whiteflies will be no problem. The result in one carefully performed experiment was simply to strangle the tomatoes with climbing nasturtium!

Mildew

Methylated spirits sprayed over the brassicas will keep them free from mildew according to one elderly gardening tome – 'if sufficient meths can be spared' was the footnote. The cynic might suggest that the use of alcohol to spray the gardener's throat so that he no longer cared about mildew might stand more chance of success. Rather more innocuous but very much more reliable, is to use soapy water as an anti-mildew spray, although it would be folly to pretend that it approaches a modern fungicide in effectiveness.

Moles

Almost anything that can generate a foul smell has been stuffed down mole tunnels in the hope of driving the pests away in disgust. Orange peel, old fish heads, paraffin, moth balls (again!) – the inventiveness of the gardening world is astounding. Few seem to have a really proven track record of success. But then neither does the growing of caper spurge in the garden have the deterrent action that is sometimes claimed for it; one well-known gardener has actually seen a caper spurge uprooted by a mole tunnelling immediately beneath it. Undoubtedly, some cats are very good at keeping down a mole population and several well-authenticated instances are known of gardens being cleared of moles simply by the owner obtaining a cat. There are, among cats, good molers and bad molers. It may be that the moles can sense when a particular cat poses a serious threat and turn on their tails as a result.

Cats

Although cats can deter moles I have never seen the reverse claimed but there are certainly occasions when the pet becomes the pest. Pepper is the traditional answer but is of very variable effectiveness and I know of two instances where curry powder was much more reliable.

Slugs

A large brick after dark is the countryman's answer to the slug problem but other, less dramatic remedies act on the principle of providing a surface texture that is a deterrent to the slugs' progress. Strands of horse-hair rope were recommended in the past but small gorse or even holly twigs are equally effective. Powdery substances such as soot or ash are often reliable too.

19. Pest and Disease Spraying Calendar

Even the most experienced of gardeners needs a memory jogger; a personal diary to remind him when to begin sowing the broad beans, of the latest date at which weedkiller should be put on his lawn and so forth. This is especially true of pest and disease control where many of the modern chemical treatments necessitate, not one, but a programme of repeat sprays for satisfactory protection. It is also important to be able to recognise the growth stage of fruit trees at which the treatments must be applied; not only so that the pest or disease is caught at its most vulnerable stage, but also in order to avoid the possibility of damage to the plants themselves or to beneficial insects and other wild-life.

Not every gardener will need to make use of all the recommendations in the following calendar but it provides systematic guidelines for combating most of the major garden problems mentioned in the book. The calendar is divided into two parts. In the monthly listing below are suggestions for pest and disease control apart from the spring and summer spraying programme on fruit trees, for which it is important to be able to identify precisely the growth stage of the plants and which will vary, not only across the country, but also between varieties and seasons. These are shown pictorially on the next page.

* All the items on the calendar identified with an asterisk should be continued routinely, either every two or three weeks or as and when symptoms reappear throughout the summer. Details of the best chemicals to use in each case are given in the main text throughout the book.

Pest and disease controls month by month

January	Clear away garden rubbish. Look out for signs of Coral Spot on old branches and twigs. Final chance to use tar oil winter washes on dormant woody plants.
February	First sprays for Peach Leaf Curl as the buds are swelling. Check that all pots, boxes, and seed trays are clean and disinfected. Check for Big Bud symptoms on blackcurrants.
March	Second spray for Peach Leaf Curl as leaves expand. *Begin to use slug controls as first plants are put out. Look out for, and pick off, first signs of mildew as fruit tree leaves unfold.
April	*Use soil insecticides when pricking out young plants. *Check routinely for aphids and whiteflies in greenhouses. *Protect brassica seedlings against flea beetle. *Protect brassica transplants against clubroot. First spray on raspberries against grey mould.
May	*Protect brassica transplants against cabbage root fly. *Check for caterpillars on all types of fruit, vegetables and ornamentals. *Begin sprays against raspberry cane midge. *Check routinely for aphids on all types of fruit, vegetables and ornamentals. *Begin sprays against rose mildew, black spot and rust.
June	Spray for pea moth control before and after flowers open. Carefully check over bulbs for pests and diseases after lifting and drying for storage.
July	Begin protective sprays against potato blight in damp seasons.
August	Check that fruit and vegetable stores are rodent proof. Buy mousetraps!
September	Check carefully all fruit intended for storage. Soak bulbs in fungicide before planting.
October	Last spray against Peach Leaf Curl as leaves drop. Apply grease bands to fruit trees to control winter moth.
November	Remove dead wood from trees and shrubs; check for and cut out any cankers. Take care not to cut too close to trunk (see page 29).
December	Apply tar oil winter wash or spray on dormant fruit trees for control of aphids and other pests overwintering in the bark.

Spray programme

This spray programme is for apples, pears and plums for the control of winter moth, codling moth, woolly aphid, aphid, sawfly, capsid bug, sucker, scab and mildew – check the text for recommended chemicals in each case. Growth stages of fruit trees can be used to identify the time to apply sprays (n.b. winter washes should be used also, in the dormant season).

Bud burst – winter moth, aphids, scab

Green cluster (omit with plums) – aphids, suckers, scab

Pink bud (or white bud on plums and pears) – mildew, scab

Petal drop – sawfly, codling moth, capsid bug, mildew, scab

Fruitlet (omit with plums) – mildew, sucker (pears only), codling moth, aphids

Young fruit – mildew, codling moth

Index

All the pests and diseases described in the book are listed at least twice; under their own name, alphabetically, and also under the name of the plant(s) that they affect. For conciseness however, it is impossible to mention every garden plant individually. A few very important types (tomatoes, for example) or those with unique problems are listed individually, yet others are grouped with similar and related forms (cabbages, cauliflowers and Brussels sprouts as Brassicas, for example) whilst for the majority, reference should be sought under the broad divisions used in the Contents listing on page 3.

Algae, lawns 21.
Aphids 59, 60, bedding plants 16, 43, brassicas 43, fruit trees 30, 61, herbaceous perennials 18, house plants 13, lettuce 43, roses 21, soft fruit 35, vegetable fruit 37.
Apples, nutritional disorders, 17. Also see Fruit Trees.

Bacteria, as a cause of disease 4.
Beans, aphids37, botrytis 36, leaf spots (anthracnose, chocolate spot, halo blight) 38, nutritional disorders 17, wilt and root rot 41.
Beetroot, leaf miners 45, nutritional disorders 17, scab 48.
Bedding Plants, aphids 16, 43, birds 14, 16, botrytis 16, 44, caterpillars 16, 42, clubroot 16, 46, cutworms 15, 16, establishment problems 16, leatherjackets 15–16, mice, 14, 18, powdery mildew 16, 44, root, stem and foot rots 16, snails 15–16, slugs 15–16, voles 14, 16, wireworms 15–16.
Big Bud, blackcurrants 32.
Biological control of pests 7, 51.
Birds, brassicas 43, fruit trees, 29, seedlings 14.
Black Leg, potatoes 49.
Blossom End Rot, tomatoes 36.
Blossom Problems, fruit trees 22, 26.
Botrytis 60, leafy vegetables 44, soft fruit 34, vegetable fruit 36, wallflowers 16, 46.
Brassicas, aphids 44, birds 44, botrytis 44, cabbage root fly 46, caterpillars 42, clubroot 46, downy mildew 44, flea beetles 47, leaf miners 44, leaf spots 42, 44, nutritional disorders 17, powdery mildew 44, rabbits 44, scab 48, soft rot 49, virus 44, whiteflies 44.
Brown Rot, fruit 27.
Brussels Sprouts. See Brassicas.
Bulbs, corms and tubers, importance of obtaining healthy stock 6, pest and disease control on 60, problems of 19, storage of 6 . Also see Herbaceous Perennials.

Cabbage. See Brassicas.
Cabbage Root Fly 60, brassicas 46.
Camellias, nutritional disorders 17
Cane Problems, soft fruit 35, 60
Canker, fruit trees 28–29, parsnip 49.
Capsid Bug, fruit trees 31, 61.
Carrot, carrot fly 47, mis-shapen roots 48.
Carrot Fly, carrot, parsnip, parsley and celery 47.
Caterpillars 60, bedding plants 16, 42, brassicas 42, fruit trees (winter moths) 26, 61, (codling moth) 31, 61, peas (pea moth) 38, 60, soft fruit (magpie moth, raspberry moth) 33, trees and shrubs 25.
Cats 59, seedlings 14–15.
Cauliflowers. See Brassicas.
Celery, carrot fly 47, leaf miners 45, leaf spots 42, nutritional disorders 17, virus 42.
Chemicals, damage to lawns by 21, damage to tomatoes by 40, for pest and disease control, safety 8, systemic and contact 9.
Chicory, nutritional disorders 17.
Clubroot 60, brassicas 46, 58, wallflowers 16, 46.
Compost, use of 7.
Coral Spot, trees and shrubs 25, 60.
Cucumbers. See Cucurbits.
Cucurbits, aphids 37, botrytis 36, whitefly 37, virus 40.
Cutworms, bedding plants 15, 16, herbaceous perennials 19, seedlings 15.

Damping Off, seedlings 14.
Deer 24.
Disease, definition 4.
Downy Mildew, brassicas 43, lettuce 43, spinach 43.

Earwigs, herbaceous perennials 18.
Eelworms, potatoes 49, 58.
Egg Plant, aphids, 37, botrytis 36, whiteflies 37.
Establishment Problems, bedding plants 16, lawns 21.

Fairy Rings, lawns 21.
Fanging and forking, roots 48.
Fireblight, fruit trees 26, trees and shrubs 21.
Flea Beetles 60, radish, swede and turnip 47.
Fruit (general) nutritional disorders 17.
Fruit (Soft) aphids 35, big bud 32, botrytis 34, caterpillars 33, leaf spots 33, powdery mildew 34, raspberry beetle 33, raspberry cane problems 35, red spider mite 34, rust 32 , virus 35.
Fruit trees, aphids 30–31 , birds 29, blossom problems 22, 26, brown rot 27, canker 28–29, capsid bug 31, codling moth 31, peach leaf curl 30 , pear leaf blister mite 27, pear midge 27, plum rust 28, powdery mildew 31, sawfly 31, scab 30, silver leaf 28, soil sickness and replant diseases 28, viruses 27, wasps 29, winter moths 26.
Fungus, as a cause of disease 4.
Fungus gnats, house plants 13.

Galls (trees) 25.
Greenhouses, in relation to pests and diseases 50–1.

Herbaceous perennials, aphids 18, cutworms 19, earwigs 18, leaf spots 18, 20, leatherjackets 19, powdery mildew 18–19, rust 18, 20, slugs and snails 18, wireworms 19.
Honey Fungus 24, 58.
House Plants, aphids 13, fungus gnats 13, mealy bugs 12, red spider mites 13, scale insects 12, vine weevil 13, whiteflies 13.
Hydrangeas, nutritional disorders 17.
Hygiene in the garden 7, in the greenhouse 50.

Insecticides 8–9.

Lawns, algae, dead patches, establishment problems, fairy rings, lichen, moles 21.
Leaf-cutter bee, rose 21.
Leaf hopper, rose 21.
Leaf miner, beetroot, brassicas, celery 42.
Leaf spots, beans 38, brassicas 42, celery 42, herbaceous perennials 18, rose (black spot) 20, 60, soft fruit 33, trees and shrubs 22.
Leafy Vegetables, aphids 43, birds 43, botrytis 43, caterpillars 42, downy mildew 43, leaf miners 43, leaf spots 42, powdery mildew 43, rabbits 43, virus 43, whitefly 43.
Leather jackets, bedding plants 15–16, herbaceous perennials 19, lawns 21, seedlings 15.

Lettuce, aphids 43, downy mildew 43, nutritional disorders 17, virus 44.
Lichens, lawns 21.

Mealy Bugs, house plants 12.
Mice, seedlings 14, in stores 53.
Mildew. See Downy Mildew and Powdery Mildew.
Millepedes, seedlings 15.
Mistletoe 23.
Moles 21, 59.

Neck Rot, onion 53.
Nutritional Disorders, general 17, tomato 40–41.

Oedema, tomato 40.
Onion, neck rot 53, white rot 47.

Pansies and violas, soil sickness 16.
Parsley, carrot fly 47.
Parsnip, canker 49, carrot fly 47, misshapen roots 48, nutritional disorders 17.
Peas, botrytis 36, nutritional disorders 17, pea moth 38, wilt and root rot 41.
Peach Leaf Curl 30, 50, 60.
Pear Leaf Blister Mite 27.
Pear Midge 27.
Peppers, aphids 37, nutritional disorders 17, whitefly 37.
Pests, types affecting garden plants 5.
Pesticides 8-9.
Phytophthora Root Death, trees and shrubs 23.
Plants, importance of buying healthy stock 6.
Potato Blight, potatoes and tomatoes 48, 60, tomato 36.
Potato, black leg 49, blight 48, eelworm 49, nutritional disorders 17, scab 48, skin spot 48, virus 48, wart 48.
Powdery Mildew 59–60, bedding plants 16, 44, brassicas 44, fruit trees 31, 61, herbaceous perennials 18–19, rose 19, soft fruit 34, trees and shrubs 25, vegetable fruit 40.

Rabbits 24.
Raspberry Beetle 33.
Red Spider Mite,house plants 13, soft fruit 34.
Resistant varieties (general) 7.
Rhododendrons, nutritional disorders 17.
Root Nodules 39.
Root Rot, tomatoes, beans and peas 41.
Root, stem and foot rots, bedding plants 16.
Roses, black spot 20, mildew 19, nutritional disorders 17, pests (aphids, leaf-cutter bee, leaf hopper, leaf-rolling sawfly) 21, rust 10, 60, soil sickness 28.
Rot and decay, trees and shrubs 23.
Rust, herbaceous perennials 18, 20, plum 28, rose 10, 60, soft fruit 32.

Sawfly, fruit trees 31, rose leaf-rolling 21.
Scab, fruit 30, 61, root vegetables 48.
Scale Insects, house plants 12.
Seedlings, birds 14, cats 14–15, cutworms 15, damping off 14, leatherjackets 15, mice 14, millepedes 15, slugs 15, snails 15, woodlice 15.
Seeds, importance of obtaining healthy stock 6, storage of 6.
Silver Leaf 28.
Skin Spot, potato 48.
Slugs, 59–60 bedding plants 15–16, herbaceous perennials 18, seedlings 15.
Smut, sweet corn 39.
Snails, bedding plants 15–16, herbaceous perennials 18, seedlings 15.
Soft Rot, root vegetables 49, vegetable fruit 36.
Soil Sickness, fruit trees, roses 28, pansies 16.
Spinach, downy mildew 43, nutritional disorders 17.
Splitting, tomatoes 41.
Sprayers, types 8–9.
Squirrels 24.
Storage, of fruit and vegetables 52–53.
Suckers (insects), fruit trees 26, 60.
Swedes, nutritional disorders 17. Also see Brassicas.
Sweet corn, smut 39.

Tomato, aphids 37, blossom end rot 36, 41, botrytis 36, ghost spot 37, leaf mould 36, leaf problems 40, nutritional disorders 17, 40–41, oedema 40 , potato blight 36, 48, soft rot 49, splitting, blackening and rotting 41, virus 40, weedkiller damage 40, whitefly 37, wilt and root rot 41.
Trees and shrubs, caterpillars 25, coral spot 25 , honey fungus 24, fireblight 22, leaf spots 22, mammals (deer, rabbits, squirrels) 24, mistletoe and unusual growths 22, powdery mildew 25, phytophthora root death 22, rot and decay 22, swellings 25.

Vegetable Fruits, aphids 37, bean spotting 38, botrytis 36, cucumber virus 40, ghost spot 37, leaf mould 36, pea moth 38, powdery mildew 40, sweet corn smut 39, splitting, blackening and rotting 41, root nodules 39, tomato leaf problems 40, wilts and root rots 41.
Vine Weevil, house plants 13.
Virus, as cause of disease 4, 7, brassicas 42, celery 42, cucurbits 40, herbaceous perennials 19, fruit trees 27, potatoes 48, soft fruit 35, tomatoes 40.

Wart, potato 48.
Wasps 9.
Whiteflies 59, 60, brassicas 45, house plants 13, vegetable fruits 37.
Wilt, tomatoes, beans, peas 41.
Wireworms, seedlings 15, bedding plants 15, 16, herbaceous perennials 19.
Witches' Brooms 23.
Woodlice 15.
Wound treatment on trees 23.

Dr Stefan Buczacki was born in Derbyshire in 1945. He obtained a First in Botany at Southampton University and a Doctorate in Forestry at Oxford before working for the Agricultural Research Council as a Plant Pathologist. He acquired an international reputation for his studies on root diseases but also developed a special interest in the communication of science to non-scientists. In addition to over seventy scientific papers and books, he is the author of innumerable popular and semi-popular articles on gardening and natural history and co-author of the highly acclaimed *Collins Guide to the Pests, Diseases and Disorders of Garden Plants*, the standard work in its field. Since 1982 he has been resident scientist on the panel of BBC *Gardeners' Question Time* and recently gave up his research post to concentrate full-time on broadcasting, writing and photography. He is married, with two sons, and lives near Stratford upon Avon.